# Essays

Charles Lamb

DODO PRESS

CONTENTS

RECOLLECTIONS OF CHRIST'S HOSPITAL

ON THE TRAGEDIES OF SHAKSPEARE, CONSIDERED WITH REFERENCE TO THEIR FITNESS FOR STAGE-REPRESENTATION

CHARACTERS OF DRAMATIC WRITERS, CONTEMPORARY WITH SHAKSPEARE

SPECIMENS FROM THE WRITINGS OF FULLER, THE CHURCH HISTORIAN

ON THE GENIUS AND CHARACTER OF HOGARTH; WITH SOME REMARKS ON APASSAGE IN THE WRITINGS OF THE LATE MR. BARRY

ON THE POETICAL WORKS OF GEORGE WITHER

# Essays

## RECOLLECTIONS OF CHRIST'S HOSPITAL.

To comfort the desponding parent with the thought that, without diminishing the stock which is imperiously demanded to furnish the more pressing and homely wants of our nature, he has disposed of one or more perhaps out of a numerous offspring, under the shelter of a care scarce less tender than the paternal, where not only their bodily cravings shall be supplied, but that mental *pabulum* is also dispensed, which HE hath declared to be no less necessary to our sustenance, who said, that, "not by bread alone man can live": for this Christ's Hospital unfolds her bounty. Here neither, on the one hand, are the youth lifted up above their family, which we must suppose liberal, though reduced; nor on the other hand, are they liable to be depressed below its level by the mean habits and sentiments which a common charity-school generates. It is, in a word, an Institution to keep those who have yet held up their heads in the world, from sinking; to keep alive the spirit of a decent household, when poverty was in danger of crushing it; to assist those who are the most willing, but not always the most able, to assist themselves; to separate a child from his family for a season, in order to render him back hereafter, with feelings and habits more congenial to it, than he could even have attained by remaining at home in the bosom of it. It is a preserving and renovating principle, an antidote for the *res angusta domi*, when it presses, as it always does, most heavily upon the most ingenuous natures.

This is Christ's Hospital; and whether its character would be improved by confining its advantages to the very lowest of the people, let those judge who have witnessed the looks, the gestures, the behavior, the manner of their play with one another, their deportment towards strangers, the whole aspect and physiognomy of that vast assemblage of boys on the London foundation, who freshen and make alive again with their sports the else mouldering cloisters of the old Grey Friars—which strangers who have never witnessed, if they pass through Newgate Street, or by Smithfield, would do well to go a little out of their way to see.

For the Christ's Hospital boy feels that he is no charity-boy; he feels it in the antiquity and regality of the foundation to which he belongs; in the usage which he meets with at school, and the treatment he is accustomed to out of its bounds; in the respect and even kindness, which his well-known garb never fails to procure him in the streets of the metropolis; he feels it in his education, in that measure of classical attainments, which every individual at that school, though not destined to a learned profession, has it in his power to procure, attainments which it would be worse than folly to put it in the reach of the laboring classes to acquire: he feels it in the numberless comforts, and even magnificences, which surround him; in his old and awful cloisters, with their traditions; in his spacious schoolrooms, and in the well-ordered, airy, and lofty rooms where he sleeps; in his stately dining-hall, hung round with pictures, by Verrio, Lely, and others, one of them surpassing in size and grandeur almost any other in the kingdom; [1] above all, in the very extent and magnitude of the body to which he belongs, and the consequent spirit, the intelligence, and public conscience, which is the result of so many various yet wonderfully combining members. Compared with this last-named advantage, what is the stock of information (I do not here speak of book-learning, but of that knowledge which boy receives from boy), the mass of collected opinions, the intelligence in common, among the few and narrow members of an ordinary boarding-school?

[Footnote 1: By Verrio, representing James the Second on his throne, surrounded by his courtiers, (all curious portraits, ) receiving the mathematical pupils at their annual presentation: a custom still kept up on New-year's-day at Court. ]

The Christ's Hospital or Blue-coat boy, has a distinctive character of his own, as far removed from the abject qualities of a common charity-boy as it is from the disgusting forwardness of a lad brought up at some other of the public schools. There is *pride* in it, accumulated from the circumstances which I have described, as differencing him from the former; and there is *a restraining modesty* from a sense of obligation and dependence, which must ever keep his deportment from assimilating to that of the latter. His very garb, as it is antique and venerable, feeds his self-respect; as it is a badge of dependence, it restrains the natural petulance of that age from breaking out into overt acts of insolence. This produces silence and a reserve before strangers, yet not that cowardly shyness which boys mewed up at home will feel; he will speak up when spoken to, but the stranger must begin the conversation with him. Within his bounds he is all fire and play; but in the streets he steals along with all the self-concentration of a young monk. He is never known to mix with other boys; they are a sort of laity to him. All this proceeds, I have no doubt, from the continual consciousness which he carries about him, of the difference of his dress from that of the rest of the world; with a modest jealousy over himself, lest, by overhastily mixing with common and secular playfellows, he should commit the dignity of his cloth. Nor let any one laugh at this; for, considering the propensity of the multitude, and especially of the small multitude, to ridicule anything unusual in dress—above all, where such peculiarity may be construed by malice into a mark of disparagement—this reserve will appear to be nothing more than a wise instinct in the Blue-coat boy. That it is neither pride nor rusticity, at least that it has none of the offensive qualities of either, a stranger may soon satisfy himself, by putting a question to any of these boys: he may be sure of an answer couched in terms of plain civility, neither loquacious nor embarrassed. Let him put the same question to a parish-boy, or to one of the trencher-caps in the — — cloisters, and the impudent reply of the one shall not fail to exasperate any more than the certain servility, and mercenary eye to reward, which he will meet with in the other, can fail to depress and sadden him.

The Christ's Hospital boy is a religions character. His school is eminently a religious foundation; it has its peculiar prayers, its services at set times, its graces, hymns, and anthems, following each other in an almost monastic closeness of succession. This religious character in him is not always untinged with superstition. That is not wonderful, when we consider the thousand tales and traditions which must circulate, with undisturbed credulity, amongst so many boys, that have so few checks to their belief from any intercourse with the world at large; upon whom their equals in age must work so much, their elders so little. With this leaning towards an over-belief in matters of religion, which will soon correct itself when he comes out into society, may be classed a turn for romance above most other boys. This is to be traced in the same manner to their excess of society with each other, and defect of mingling with the world. Hence the peculiar avidity with which such books as the "Arabian Nights' Entertainments, " and others of a still wilder cast, are, or at least were in my time, sought for by the boys. I remember when some half-dozen of them set off from school, without map, card, or compass, on a serious expedition to find out *Philip Quarll's Island*.

The Christ's Hospital boy's sense of right and wrong is peculiarly tender and apprehensive. It is even apt to run out into ceremonial observances, and to impose a yoke upon itself beyond the strict obligations of the moral law. Those who were contemporaries with me at that school thirty years ago, will remember with what more than Judaic rigor the eating of the fat of certain boiled meats[1] was interdicted. A boy would have blushed as at the exposure of some heinous immorality, to have been detected eating that forbidden portion of his allowance of animal food, the whole of which, while he was in health, was little more than sufficient to allay his hunger. The same, or even greater, refinement was shown in the rejection of certain kinds of sweet-cake. What gave rise to these supererogatory penances, these self-denying ordinances, I could never learn; [2] they certainly argue no defect of the conscientious principle. A little excess in that article is not undesirable in youth, to make allowance for the inevitable waste which comes in maturer years. But in the less ambiguous line of duty, in those directions of the moral feelings which cannot be mistaken or depreciated, I will relate what took place in the year 1785, when Mr. Perry, the steward, died. I must be pardoned for taking my instances from my own times. Indeed, the vividness of my recollections, while I am upon this subject, almost bring back those times; they are present to me still. But I believe that in the years which have elapsed since the period which I speak of, the character of the Christ's Hospital boy is very little changed. Their situation in point of many comforts is improved; but that which I ventured before to term the *public conscience* of the school, the pervading moral sense, of which every mind partakes and to which so many individual minds contribute, remains, I believe, pretty much the same as when I left it. I have seen, within this twelvemonth almost, the change which has been produced upon a boy of eight or nine years of age, upon being admitted into that school; how, from a pert young coxcomb, who thought that all knowledge was comprehended within his shallow brains, because a smattering of two or three languages and one or two sciences were stuffed into him by injudicious treatment at home, by a mixture with the wholesome society of so many school-fellows, in less time than I have spoken of, he has sunk to his own level, and is contented to be carried on in the quiet orbit of modest self-knowledge in which the common mass of that unpresumptuous assemblage of boys seem to move: from being a little unfeeling mortal, he has got to feel and reflect. Nor would it be a difficult matter to show how, at a school like this, where the boy is neither entirely separated from home, nor yet exclusively under its influence, the best feelings, the filial for instance, are brought to a maturity which they could not have attained under a completely domestic education; how the relation of a parent is rendered less tender by unremitted association, and the very awfulness of age is best apprehended by some sojourning amidst the comparative levity of youth; how absence, not drawn out by too great extension into alienation or forgetfulness, puts an edge upon the relish of occasional intercourse, and the boy is made the better *child* by that which keeps the force of that relation from being felt as perpetually pressing on him; how the substituted paternity, into the care of which he is adopted, while in everything substantial it makes up for the natural, in the necessary omission of individual fondnesses and partialities, directs the mind only the more strongly to appreciate that natural and first tie, in which such weaknesses are the bond of strength, and the appetite which craves after them betrays no perverse palate. But these speculations rather belong to the question of the comparative advantages of a public over a private education in general. I must get back to my favorite school; and to that which took place when our old and good steward died.

[Footnote 1: Under the denomination of *gage*. ]

[Footnote 2: I am told that the late steward [Mr. Hathaway], who evinced on many occasions a most praiseworthy anxiety to promote the comfort of the boys, had occasion for all his address and perseverance to eradicate the first of these unfortunate prejudices, in which he at length happily succeeded, and thereby restored to one half of the animal nutrition of the school those honors which painful superstition and blind zeal had so long conspired to withhold from it. ]

And I will say that when I think of the frequent instances which I have met with in children, of a hard-heartedness, a callousness, and insensibility to the loss of relations, even of those who have begot and nourished them, I cannot but consider it as a proof of something in the peculiar conformation of that school, favorable to the expansion of the best feelings of our nature, that at the period which I am noticing, out of five hundred boys there was not a dry eye to be found among them, nor a heart that did not beat with genuine emotion. Every impulse to play, until the funeral day was past, seemed suspended throughout the school; and the boys, lately so mirthful and sprightly, were seen pacing their cloisters alone, or in sad groups standing about, few of them without some token, such as their slender means could provide, a black riband or something, to denote respect and a sense of their loss. The time itself was a time of anarchy, a time in which all authority (out of school hours) was abandoned. The ordinary restraints were for those days superseded;

and the gates, which at other times kept us in, were left without watchers. Yet, with the exception of one or two graceless boys at most, who took advantage of that suspension of authorities to *skulk out*, as it was called, the whole body of that great school kept rigorously within their bounds, by a voluntary self-imprisonment; and they who broke bounds, though they escaped punishment from any master, fell into a general disrepute among us, and, for that which at any other time would have been applauded and admired as a mark of spirit, were consigned to infamy and reprobation; so much *natural government* have gratitude and the principles of reverence and love, and so much did a respect to their dead friend prevail with these Christ's Hospital boys, above any fear which his presence among them when living could ever produce. And if the impressions which were made on my mind so long ago are to be trusted, very richly did their steward deserve this tribute. It is a pleasure to me even now to call to mind his portly form, the regal awe which he always contrived to inspire, in spite of a tenderness and even weakness of nature that would have enfeebled the reins of discipline in any other master; a yearning of tenderness towards those under his protection, which could make five hundred boys at once feel towards him each as to their individual father. He had faults, with which we had nothing to do; but, with all his faults, indeed, Mr. Perry was a most extraordinary creature. Contemporary with him and still living, though he has long since resigned his occupation, will it be impertinent to mention the name of our excellent upper grammar-master, the Rev. James Boyer? He was a disciplinarian, indeed, of a different stamp from him whom I have just described; but, now the terrors of the rod, and of a temper a little too hasty to leave the more nervous of us quite at our ease to do justice to his merits in those days, are long since over, ungrateful were we if we should refuse our testimony to that unwearied assiduity with which he attended to the particular improvement of each of us. Had we been the offspring of the first gentry in the land, he could not have been instigated by the strongest views of recompense and reward to have made himself a greater slave to the most laborious of all occupations than he did for us sons of charity, from whom, or from our parents, he could expect nothing. He has had his reward in the satisfaction of having discharged his duty, in the pleasurable consciousness of having advanced the respectability of that institution to which, both man and boy, he was attached; in the honors to which so many of his pupils have successfully aspired at both our Universities; and in the staff with which the Governors of the Hospital, at the close of his hard labors, with the highest expressions of the obligations the school lay under to him, unanimously voted to present him.

I have often considered it among the felicities of the constitution of this school, that the offices of steward and school-master are kept distinct; the strict business of education alone devolving upon the latter, while the former has the charge of all things out of school, the control of the provisions, the regulation of meals, of dress, of play, and the ordinary intercourse of the boys. By this division of management, a superior respectability must attach to the teacher, while his office is unmixed with any of these lower concerns. A still greater advantage over the construction of common boarding-schools is to be found in the settled salaries of the masters, rendering them totally free of obligation to any individual pupil, or his parents. This never fails to have its effect at schools where each boy can reckon up to a hair what profit the master derives from him, where he views him every day in the light of a caterer, a provider for the family, who is to get so much by him in each of his meals. Boys will see and consider these things; and how much must the sacred character of preceptor suffer in their minds by these degrading associations! The very bill which the pupil carries home with him at Christmas, eked out, perhaps, with elaborate though necessary minuteness, instructs him that his teachers have other ends than the mere love to learning, in the lessons which they give him; and though they put into his hands the fine sayings of Seneca or Epictetus, yet they themselves are none of those disinterested pedagogues to teach philosophy *gratis*. The master, too, is sensible that he is seen in this light; and how much this must lessen that affectionate regard to the learners which alone can sweeten the bitter labor of instruction, and convert the whole business into unwelcome and uninteresting task-work, many preceptors that I have conversed with on the subject are ready, with a sad heart, to acknowledge. From this inconvenience the settled salaries of the masters of this school in great measure exempt them; while the happy custom of choosing masters (indeed every officer of the establishment) from those who have received their education there, gives them an interest in advancing the character of the school, and binds them to observe a tenderness and a respect to the children, in which a stranger, feeling that independence which I have spoken of, might well be expected to fail.

In affectionate recollections of the place where he was bred up, in hearty recognitions of old school-fellows met with again after the lapse of years, or in foreign countries, the Christ's Hospital boy yields to none; I might almost say, he goes beyond most other boys. The very compass and magnitude of the school, its thousand bearings, the space it takes up in the imagination beyond the ordinary schools, impresses a remembrance, accompanied with an elevation of mind, that attends him through life. It is too big, too affecting an object, to pass away quickly from his mind. The Christ's Hospital boy's friends at school are commonly his intimates through life. For me, I do not know whether a constitutional imbecility does not incline me too obstinately to cling to the remembrances of childhood; in an inverted ratio to the usual sentiments of mankind, nothing that I have been engaged in since seems of any value or importance compared to the colors which imagination gave to everything then. I belong to no *body corporate* such as I then made a part of. —And here, before I close, taking leave of the general reader, and addressing myself solely to my old school-fellows, that were contemporaries with me from the year 1782 to 1789, let me have leave to remember some of those circumstances of our school, which they will not be unwilling to have brought back to their minds.

And first, let us remember, as first in importance in our childish eyes, the young men (as they almost were) who, under the denomination of *Grecians*, were waiting the expiration of the period when they should be sent, at the charges of the Hospital, to one or other of our universities, but more frequently to Cambridge. These youths, from their superior acquirements, their superior age and stature, and the fewness of their numbers (for seldom above two or three at a time were inaugurated into that high order), drew the eyes of all, and especially of the younger boys, into a reverent observance and admiration. How tall they used to seem to us! how stately would they pace along the cloisters! while the play of the lesser boys was absolutely suspended, or its boisterousness at least allayed, at their presence! Not that they ever beat or struck the boys—that would have been to have demeaned themselves—the dignity of their persons alone insured them all respect. The task of blows, of corporal chastisement, they left to the common monitors, or heads of wards, who, it must be confessed, in our time had rather too much license allowed them to oppress and misuse their inferiors; and the interference of the Grecian, who may be considered as the spiritual power, was not unfrequently called for, to mitigate by its mediation the heavy unrelenting arm of this temporal power, or monitor. In fine, the Grecians were the solemn Muftis of the school. Eras were computed from their time; —it used to be said, such or such a thing was done when S— — or T— — was Grecian.

As I ventured to call the Grecians, the Muftis of the school, the King's boys, [1] as their character then was, may well pass for the Janissaries. They were the terror of all the other boys; bred up under that hardy sailor, as well as excellent mathematician and conavigator with Captain Cook, William Wales. All his systems were adapted to fit them for the rough element which they were destined to encounter. Frequent and severe punishments which were expected to be borne with more than Spartan fortitude, came to be considered less as inflictions of disgrace than as trials of obstinate endurance. To make his boys hardy, and to give them early sailor-habits, seemed to be his only aim; to this everything was subordinate. Moral obliquities, indeed, were sure of receiving their full recompense, for no occasion of laying on the lash was ever let slip; but the effects expected to be produced from it were something very different from contrition or mortification. There was in William Wales a perpetual fund of humor, a constant glee about him, which, heightened by an inveterate provincialism of north-country dialect, absolutely took away the sting from his severities. His punishments were a game at patience, in which the master was not always worst contented when he found himself at times overcome by his pupil. What success this discipline had, or how the effects of it operated upon the after-lives of these King's boys, I cannot say: but I am sure that, for the time, they were absolute nuisances to the rest of the school. Hardy, brutal, and often wicked, they were the most graceless lump in the whole mass; older and bigger than the other boys, (for, by the system of their education they were kept longer at school by two or three years than any of the rest, except the Grecians, ) they were a constant terror to the younger part of the school; and some who may read this, I doubt not, will remember the consternation into which the juvenile fry of us were thrown, when the cry was raised in the cloisters, that *the First Order was coming*—for so they termed the first form or class of those boys. Still these sea-boys answered some good purposes, in the school. They were the military class among the boys, foremost in athletic exercises, who extended the fame of the prowess of the school far and near; and the apprentices in the vicinage, and sometimes the butchers' boys in the neighboring market, had sad occasion to attest their valor.

[Footnote 1: The mathematical pupils, bred up to the sea, on the foundation of Charles the Second. ]

The time would fail me if I were to attempt to enumerate all those circumstances, some pleasant, some attended with some pain, which, seen through the mist of distance, come sweetly softened to the memory. But I must crave leave to remember our transcending superiority in those invigorating sports, leap-frog, and basting the bear; our delightful excursions in the summer holidays to the New River, near Newington, where, like otters, we would live the long day in the water, never caring for dressing ourselves, when we had once stripped; our savory meals afterwards, when we came home almost famished with staying out all day without our dinners; our visits at other times to the Tower, where, by ancient privilege, we had free access to all the curiosities; our solemn procession through the City at Easter, with the Lord Mayor's largess of buns, wine, and a shilling, with the festive questions and civic pleasantries of the dispensing Aldermen, which were more to us than all the rest of the banquet; our stately suppings in public, where the well-lighted hall and the confluence of well-dressed company who came to see us, made the whole look more like a concert or assembly, than a scene of a plain bread and cheese collation; the annual orations upon St. Matthew's day, in which the senior scholar, before he had done, seldom failed to reckon up, among those who had done honor to our school by being educated in it, the names of those accomplished critics and Greek scholars, Joshua Barnes and Jeremiah Markland (I marvel they left out Camden while they were about it). Let me have leave to remember our hymns and anthems, and well-toned organ; the doleful tune of the burial anthem chanted in the solemn cloisters, upon the seldom-occurring funeral of some school-fellow; the festivities at Christmas, when the richest of us would club our stock to have a gaudy day, sitting round the fire, replenished to the height with logs, and the penniless, and he that could contribute nothing, partook in all the mirth, and in some of the substantialities of the feasting; the carol sung by night at that time of the year, which, when a young boy, I have so often lain awake to hear from seven (the hour of going to bed) till ten, when it was sung by the older boys and monitors, and have listened to it, in their rude chanting, till I have been transported in fancy to the fields of Bethlehem, and the song which was sung at that season, by angels' voices to the shepherds.

Nor would I willingly forget any of those things which administered to our vanity. The hem-stitched bands and town-made shirts, which some of the most fashionable among us wore; the town-girdles, with buckles of silver, or shining stone; the badges of the sea-boys; the cots, or superior shoestrings, of the monitors; the medals of the markers; (those who were appointed to hear the Bible read in the wards on Sunday morning and evening, ) which bore on their obverse in silver, as certain parts of our garments carried, in meaner metal, the countenance of our Founder, that godly and royal child, King Edward the Sixth, the flower of the Tudor name—the young flower that was untimely cropt, as it began to fill our land with its early odors—the boy-patron of boys—the serious and holy child who walked with Cranmer and Bidley—fit associate, in those tender years, for the bishops, and future martyrs of our Church, to receive, or, (as occasion sometimes proved, ) to give instruction.

"But, ah! what means the silent tear?
  Why, e'en 'mid joy, my bosom heave?
Ye long-lost scenes, enchantments dear!
  Lo! now I linger o'er your grave.

"—Fly, then, ye hours of rosy hue,
  And bear away the bloom of years!
And quick succeed, ye sickly crew
  Of doubts and sorrows, pains and fears!

"Still will I ponder Fate's unaltered plan,
Nor, tracing back the child, forget that I am man."[1]

[Footnote 1: Lines meditated in the cloisters of Christ's Hospital, in the "Poetics, " of Mr. George Dyer. ]

Essays

## ON THE TRAGEDIES OF SHAKSPEARE.

### CONSIDERED WITH REFERENCE TO THEIR FITNESS FOR STAGE-REPRESENTATION.

Taking a turn the other day in the Abbey, I was struck with the affected attitude of a figure, which I do not remember to have seen before, and which upon examination proved to be a whole-length of the celebrated Mr. Garrick. Though I would not go so far with some good Catholics abroad as to shut players altogether out of consecrated ground, yet I own I was not a little scandalized at the introduction of theatrical airs and gestures into a place set apart to remind us of the saddest realities. Going nearer, I found inscribed under this harlequin figure the following lines: —

"To paint fair Nature, by divine command
Her magic pencil in his glowing hand,
A Shakspeare rose; then, to expand his fame
Wide o'er this breathing world, a Garrick came.
Though sunk in death the forms the Poet drew,
The Actor's genius bade them breathe anew;
Though, like the bard himself, in night they lay,
Immortal Garrick called them back to day:
And till Eternity with power sublime
Shall mark the mortal hour of hoary Time,
Shakspeare and Garrick like twin-stars shall shine,
And earth irradiate with a beam divine."

It would be an insult to my readers' understandings to attempt anything like a criticism on this farrago of false thoughts and nonsense. But the reflection it led me into was a kind of wonder, how, from the days of the actor here celebrated to our own, it should have been the fashion to compliment every performer in his turn, that has had the luck to please the Town in any of the great characters of Shakspeare, with the notion of possessing a *mind congenial with the poet's*; how people should come thus unaccountably to confound the power of originating poetical images and conceptions with the faculty of being able to read or recite the same when put into words; [1]or what connection that absolute mastery over the heart and soul of man, which a great dramatic poet possesses, has with those low tricks upon the eye and ear, which a player, by observing a few general effects, which some common passion, as grief, anger, &c., usually has upon the gestures and exterior, can so easily compass. To know the internal workings and movements of a great mind, of an Othello or a Hamlet for instance, the *when* and the *why* and the *how far* they should be moved; to what pitch a passion is becoming; to give the reins and to pull in the curb exactly at the moment when the drawing in or the slackening is most graceful; seems to demand a reach of intellect of a vastly different extent from that which is employed upon the bare imitation of the signs of these passions in the countenance or gesture, which signs are usually observed to be most lively and emphatic in the weaker sort of minds, and which signs can after all but indicate some passion, as I said before, anger, or grief, generally; but of the motives and grounds of the passion, wherein it differs from the same passion in low and vulgar natures, of these the actor can give no more idea by his face or gesture than the eye (without a metaphor) can speak, or the muscles utter intelligible sounds. But such is the instantaneous nature of the impressions which we take in at the eye and ear at a playhouse, compared with the slow apprehension oftentimes of the understanding in reading, that we are apt not only to sink the playwriter in the consideration which we pay to the actor, but even to identify in our minds, in a perverse manner, the actor with the character which he represents. It is difficult for a frequent play-goer to disembarrass the idea of Hamlet from the person and voice of Mr. K. We speak of Lady Macbeth, while we are in reality thinking of Mrs. S. Nor is this confusion incidental alone to unlettered persons, who, not possessing the advantage of reading, are necessarily dependent upon the stage-player for all the pleasure which they can receive from the drama, and to whom the very idea of *what an author is* cannot be made comprehensible without some pain and perplexity of mind: the error is one from which persons otherwise not meanly lettered, find it almost impossible to extricate themselves.

[Footnote 1: It is observable that we fall into this confusion only in dramatic recitations. We never dream that the gentleman who reads Lucretius in public with great applause, is therefore a great poet and philosopher; nor do we find that Tom Davis, the bookseller, who is recorded to have recited the Paradise Lost better than any man in England in his day (though I cannot help thinking there must be some mistake in this tradition), was therefore, by his intimate friends, set upon a level with Milton. ]

Never let me be so ungrateful as to forget the very high degree of satisfaction which I received some years back from seeing for the first time a tragedy of Shakespeare performed, in which those two great performers sustained the principal parts. It seemed to embody and realize conceptions which had hitherto assumed no distinct shape. But dearly do we pay all our life after for this juvenile pleasure, this sense of distinctness. When the novelty is past, we find to our cost that instead of realizing an idea, we have only materialized and brought down a fine vision to the standard of flesh and blood. We have let go a dream, in quest of an unattainable substance.

How cruelly this operates upon the mind, to have its free conceptions thus cramped and pressed down to the measure of a strait-lacing actuality, may be judged from that delightful sensation of freshness, with which we turn to those plays of Shakspeare which have escaped being performed, and to those passages in the acting plays of the same writer which have happily been left out in the performance. How far the very custom of hearing anything *spouted*, withers and blows upon a fine passage, may be seen in those speeches from Henry the Fifth, &c., which are current in the mouths of school-boys, from their being to be found in *Enfield's Speaker*, and such kind of books! I confess myself utterly unable to appreciate that celebrated soliloquy in Hamlet, beginning "To be or not to be, " or to tell whether it be good, bad or indifferent, it has been so handled and pawed about by declamatory boys and men, and torn so inhumanly from its living place and principle of continuity in the play, till it is become to me a perfect dead member.

It may seem a paradox, but I cannot help being of opinion that the plays of Shakspeare are less calculated for performance on a stage, than those of almost any other dramatist whatever. Their distinguishing excellence is a reason that they should be so. There is so much in them, which comes not under the province of acting, with which eye, and tone, and gesture, have nothing to do.

The glory of the scenic art is to personate passion, and the turns of passion; and the more coarse and palpable the passion is, the more hold upon the eyes and ears of the spectators the performer obviously possesses. For this reason, scolding scenes, scenes where two persons talk themselves into a fit of fury, and then in a surprising manner talk themselves out of it again, have always been the most popular upon our stage. And the reason is plain, because the spectators are here most palpably appealed to, they are the proper judges in this war of words, they are the legitimate ring that should be formed round such "intellectual prize-fighters. " Talking is the direct object of the imitation here. But in all the best dramas, and in Shakspeare above all, how obvious it is, that the form of *speaking*, whether it be in soliloquy or dialogue, is only a medium, and often a highly artificial one, for putting the reader or spectator into possession of that knowledge of the inner structure and workings of mind in a character, which he could otherwise never have arrived at *in that form of composition* by any gift short of intuition. We do here as we do with novels written in the *epistolary form*. How many improprieties, perfect solecisms in letter-writing, do we put up with in Clarissa and other books, for the sake of the delight which that form upon the whole gives us!

But the practice of stage-representation reduces everything to a controversy of elocution. Every character, from the boisterous blasphemings of Bajazet to the shrinking timidity of womanhood, must play the orator. The love dialogues of Romeo and Juliet, those silver-sweet sounds of lovers' tongues by night! the more intimate and sacred sweetness of nuptial colloquy between an Othello or a Posthumus with their married wives, all those delicacies which are so delightful in the reading, as when we read of those youthful dalliances in Paradise—

"As beseem'd
Fair couple link'd in happy nuptial league,
Alone;"

by the inherent fault of stage-representation, how are these things sullied and turned from their very nature by being exposed to a large assembly; when such speeches as Imogen addresses to her lord, come drawling out of the mouth of a hired actress, whose courtship, though nominally addressed to the personated Posthumus, is manifestly aimed at the spectators, who are to judge of her endearments and her returns of love!

The character of Hamlet is perhaps that by which, since the days of Betterton, a succession of popular performers have had the greatest ambition to distinguish themselves. The length of the part may be one of their reasons. But for the character itself, we find it in a play, and therefore we judge it a fit subject of dramatic representation. The play itself abounds in maxims and reflections beyond any other, and therefore we consider it as a proper vehicle for conveying moral instruction. But Hamlet himself—what does he suffer meanwhile by being dragged forth as the public schoolmaster, to give lectures to the crowd! Why, nine parts in ten of what Hamlet does, are transactions between himself and his moral sense; they are the effusions of his solitary musings, which he retires to holes and corners and the most sequestered parts of the palace to pour forth; or rather, they are the silent meditations with which his bosom is bursting, reduced to *words* for the sake of the reader, who must else remain ignorant of what is passing there. These profound sorrows, these light-and-noise-abhorring ruminations, which the tongue scarce dares utter to deaf walls and chambers, how can they be represented by a gesticulating actor, who comes and mouths them out before an audience, making four hundred people his confidants at once! I say not that it is the fault of the actor so to do; he must pronounce them *ore rotundo*; he must accompany them with his eye; he must insinuate them into his auditory by some trick of eye, tone or gesture, or he fails. *He must be thinking all the while of his appearance, because he knows that all the while the spectators are judging of it*. And this is the way to represent the shy, negligent, retiring Hamlet!

It is true that there is no other mode of conveying a vast quantity of thought and feeling to a great portion of the audience, who otherwise would never earn it for themselves by reading, and the intellectual acquisition gained this way may, for aught I know, be inestimable; but I am not arguing that Hamlet should not be acted, but how much Hamlet is made another thing by being acted. I have heard much of the wonders which Garrick performed in this part; but as I never saw him, I must have leave to doubt whether the representation of such a character came within the province of his art. Those who tell me of him, speak of his eye, of the magic of his eye, and of his commanding voice: physical properties, vastly desirable in an actor, and without which he can never insinuate meaning into an auditory, —but what have they to do with Hamlet; what have they to do with intellect? In fact, the things aimed at in theatrical representation, are to arrest the spectator's eye upon the form and the gesture, and so to gain a more favorable hearing to what is spoken: it is not what the character is, but how he looks; not what he says, but how he speaks it. I see no reason to think that if the play of Hamlet were written over again by some such writer as Banks or Lillo, retaining the process of the story, but totally omitting all the poetry of it, all the divine features of Shakspeare, his stupendous intellect; and only taking care to give us enough of passionate dialogue, which Banks or Lillo were never at a loss to furnish; I see not how the effect could be much different upon an audience, nor how the actor has it in his power to represent Shakspeare to us differently from his representation of Banks or Lillo. Hamlet would still be a youthful accomplished prince, and must be gracefully personated; he might be puzzled in his mind, wavering in his conduct, seemingly cruel to Ophelia; he might see a ghost, and start at it, and address it kindly when he found it to be his father; all this in the poorest and most homely language of the servilest creeper after nature that ever consulted the palate of an audience; without troubling Shakspeare for the matter: and I see not but there would be room for all the power which an actor has, to display itself. All the passions and changes of passion might remain: for those are much less difficult to write or act than is thought; it is a trick easy to be attained, it is but rising or falling a note or two in the voice, a whisper with a significant foreboding look to announce its approach, and so contagious the counterfeit appearance of any emotion is, that let the words be what they will, the look and tone shall carry it off, and make it pass for deep skill in the passions.

It is common for people to talk of Shakspeare's plays being *so natural*; that everybody can understand him. They are natural indeed, they are grounded deep in nature, so deep that the depth of them lies out of the reach of most of us. You shall hear the same persons say that George Barnwell is very natural, and Othello is very natural, that they are both very deep; and to them they are the same kind of thing. At the one they sit and shed tears, because a good sort of young man is tempted by a naughty woman to commit a *trifling peccadillo*, the murder of an uncle or so[1] that is all, and so comes to an untimely end, which is *so moving*; and at the other, because a blackamoor in a fit of jealousy kills his innocent white wife; and the odds are that ninety-nine out of a hundred would willingly behold the same catastrophe happen to both the heroes, and have thought the rope more due to Othello than to Barnwell. For of the texture of Othello's mind, the inward construction marvellously laid open with all its strengths and weaknesses, its heroic confidences and its human misgivings, its agonies of hate springing from the depths of love, they see no more than the spectators at a cheaper rate, who pay their pennies apiece to look through the man's telescope in Leicester-fields, see into the inward plot and topography of the moon. Some dim thing or other they see; they see an actor personating a passion, of grief, or anger, for instance, and they recognize it as a copy of the usual external effects of such passions; or at least as being true to *that symbol of the emotion which passes current at the theatre for it*, for it is often no more than that: but of the grounds of the passion, its correspondence to a great or heroic nature, which is the only worthy object of tragedy, —that common auditors know anything of this, or can have any such notions dinned into them by the mere strength of an actor's lungs, —that apprehensions foreign to them should be thus infused into them by storm, I can neither believe, nor understand how it can be possible.

[Footnote 1: If this note could hope to meet the eye of any of the Managers, I would entreat and beg of them, in the name of both the Galleries, that this insult upon the morality of the common people of London should cease to be eternally repeated in the holiday weeks. Why are the 'Prentices of this famous and well-governed city, instead of an amusement, to be treated over and over again with a nauseous sermon of George Barnwell? Why *at the end of their vistas* are we to place the *gallows*? Were I an uncle, I should not much like a nephew of mine to have such an example placed before his eyes. It is really making uncle-murder too trivial to exhibit it as done upon such slight motives; —it is attributing too much to such characters as Millwood: —it is putting things into the heads of good young men, which they would never otherwise have dreamed of. Uncles that think anything of their lives, should fairly petition the Chamberlain against it. ]

We talk of Shakspeare's admirable observations of life, when we should feel, that not from a petty inquisition into those cheap and every-day characters which surrounded him, as they surround us, but from his own mind, which was, to borrow a phrase of Ben Jonson's, the very "sphere of humanity, " he fetched those images of virtue and of knowledge, of which every one of us recognizing a part, think we comprehend in our natures the whole; and oftentimes mistake the powers which he positively creates in us, for nothing more than indigenous faculties of our own minds, which only waited the application of corresponding virtues in him to return a full and clear echo of the same.

To return to Hamlet. —Among the distinguishing features of that wonderful character, one of the most interesting (yet painful) is that soreness of mind which makes him treat the intrusions of Polonius with harshness, and that asperity which he puts on in his interviews with Ophelia. These tokens of an unhinged mind (if they be not mixed in the latter case with a profound artifice of love, to alienate Ophelia by affected discourtesies, so to prepare her mind for the breaking off of that loving intercourse, which can no longer find a place amidst business so serious as that which he has to do) are parts of his character, which to reconcile with our admiration of Hamlet, the most patient consideration of his situation is no more than necessary; they are what we *forgive afterwards*, and explain by the whole of his character, but *at the time* they are harsh and unpleasant. Yet such is the actor's necessity of giving strong blows to the audience, that I have never seen a player in this character, who did not exaggerate and strain to the utmost these ambiguous features, — these temporary deformities in the character. They make him express a vulgar scorn at Polonius which utterly degrades his gentility, and which no explanation can render palatable; they make him show contempt, and curl up the nose at Ophelia's father, —contempt in its very grossest and most hateful form; but they get applause by it: it is natural, people say; that is, the words are scornful, and the actor expresses scorn, and that they can judge of: but why so much scorn, and of that sort, they never think of asking.

So to Ophelia. —All the Hamlets that I have ever seen, rant and rave at her as if she had committed some great crime, and the audience are highly pleased, because the words of the part are satirical, and they are enforced by the strongest expression of satirical indignation of which the face and voice are capable. But then, whether Hamlet is likely to have put on such brutal appearances to a lady whom he loved so dearly, is never thought on. The truth is, that in all such deep affections as had subsisted between Hamlet and Ophelia, there is a stock of *supererogatory love*, (if I may venture to use the expression, ) which in any great grief of heart, especially where that which preys upon the mind cannot be communicated, confers a kind of indulgence upon the grieved party to express itself, even to its heart's dearest object, in the language of a temporary alienation; but it is not alienation, it is a distraction purely, and so it always makes itself to be felt by that object: it is not anger, but grief assuming the appearance of anger, —love awkwardly counterfeiting hate, as sweet countenances when they try to frown: but such sternness and fierce disgust as Hamlet is made to show, is no counterfeit, but the real face of absolute aversion, —of irreconcilable alienation. It may be said he puts on the madman; but then he should only so far put on this counterfeit lunacy as his own real distraction will give him leave; that is, incompletely, imperfectly; not in that confirmed, practised way, like a master of his art, or as Dame Quickly would say, "like one of those harlotry players."

# Essays

I mean no disrespect to any actor, but the sort of pleasure which Shakspeare's plays give in the acting seems to me not at all to differ from that which the audience receive from those of other writers; and, *they being in themselves essentially so different from all others*, I must conclude that there is something in the nature of acting which levels all distinctions. And, in fact, who does not speak indifferently of the Gamester and of Macbeth as fine stage-performances, and praise the Mrs. Beverley in the same way as the Lady Macbeth of Mrs. S.? Belvidera, and Calista, and Isabella, and Euphrasia, are they less liked than Imogen, or than Juliet, or than Desdemona? Are they not spoken of and remembered in the same way? Is not the female performer as great (as they call it) in one as in the other? Did not Garrick shine, and was he not ambitious of shining, in every drawling tragedy that his wretched day produced, —the productions of the Hills, and the Murphys, and the Browns, —and shall he have that honor to dwell in our minds forever as an inseparable concomitant with Shakspeare? A kindred mind! O who can read that affecting sonnet of Shakspeare which alludes to his profession as a player: —

"Oh for my sake do you with Fortune chide,
The guilty goddess of my harmless deeds,
That did not better for my life provide
Than public means which public custom breeds—
Thence comes it that my name receives a brand;
And almost thence my nature is subdued
To what it works in, like the dyer's hand." —

Or that other confession: —

"Alas! 'tis true, I have gone here and there,
And made myself a motley to thy view,
Gored mine own thoughts, sold cheap what is most dear—"

Who can read these instances of jealous self-watchfulness in our sweet Shakspeare, and dream of any congeniality between him and one that, by every tradition of him, appears to have been as mere a player as ever existed; to have had his mind tainted with the lowest players' vices, —envy and jealousy, and miserable cravings after applause; one who in the exercise of his profession was jealous even of the women-performers that stood in his way; a manager full of managerial tricks and stratagems and finesse; that any resemblance should be dreamed of between him and Shakspeare, —Shakspeare, who, in the plenitude and consciousness of his own powers, could with that noble modesty, which we can neither imitate nor appreciate, express himself thus of his own sense of his own defects: —

"Wishing me like to one more rich in hope,
Featured like him, like him with friends possest;
Desiring *this man's art, and that man's scope.*"

I am almost disposed to deny to Garrick the merit of being an admirer of Shakspeare? A true lover of his excellences he certainly was not; for would any true lover of them have admitted into his matchless scenes such ribald trash as Tate and Cibber, and the rest of them, that

"With their darkness durst affront his light, "

have foisted into the acting plays of Shakspeare? I believe it impossible that he could have had a proper reverence for Shakspeare, and have condescended to go through that interpolated scene in Richard the Third, in which Richard tries to break his wife's heart by telling her he loves another woman, and says, "if she survives this she is immortal. " Yet I doubt not he delivered this vulgar stuff with as much anxiety of emphasis as any of the genuine parts: and for acting, it is as well calculated as any. But we have seen the part of Richard lately produce great fame to an actor by his manner of playing it; and it lets us into the secret of acting, and of popular judgments of Shakspeare derived from acting. Not one of the spectators who have witnessed Mr. C.'s exertions in that part, but has come away with a proper conviction that Richard is a very wicked man, and kills little children in their beds, with something like the pleasure which the giants and ogres in children's books are represented to have taken in that practice; moreover, that he is very close and shrewd, and devilish cunning, for you could see that by his eye.

But is, in fact, this the impression we have in reading the Richard of Shakspeare? Do we feel anything like disgust, as we do at that butcherlike representation of him that passes for him on the stage? A horror at his crimes blends with the effect which we feel, but how is it qualified, how is it carried off, by the rich intellect which he displays, his resources, his wit, his buoyant spirits, his vast knowledge and insight into characters, the poetry of his part, —not an atom of all which is made perceivable in Mr. C.'s way of acting it.

Nothing but his crimes, his actions, is visible; they are prominent and staring; the murderer stands out, but where is the lofty genius, the man of vast capacity, —the profound, the witty, accomplished Richard?

The truth is, the characters of Shakspeare are so much the objects of meditation rather than of interest or curiosity as to their actions, that while we are reading any of his great criminal characters, — Macbeth, Richard, even Iago, —we think not so much of the crimes which they commit, as of the ambition, the aspiring spirit, the intellectual activity, which prompts them to overleap these moral fences. Barnwell is a wretched murderer; there is a certain fitness between his neck and the rope; he is the legitimate heir to the gallows; nobody who thinks at all can think of any alleviating circumstances in his case to make him a fit object of mercy. Or to take an instance from the higher tragedy, what else but a mere assassin is Glenalvon? Do we think of anything but of the crime which he commits, and the rack which he deserves? That is all which we really think about him. Whereas in corresponding characters in Shakspeare, so little do the actions comparatively affect us, that while the impulses, the inner mind in all its perverted greatness, solely seems real and is exclusively attended to, the crime is comparatively nothing. But when we see these things represented, the acts which they do are comparatively everything, their impulses nothing. The state of sublime emotion into which we are elevated by those images of night and horror which Macbeth is made to utter, that solemn prelude with which he entertains the time till the bell shall strike which is to call him to murder Duncan, —when we no longer read it in a book, when we have given up that vantage ground of abstraction which reading possesses over seeing, and come to see a man in his bodily shape before our eyes actually preparing to commit a murder, if the acting be true and impressive, as I have witnessed it in Mr. K.'s performance of that part, the painful anxiety about the act, the natural longing to prevent it while it yet seems unperpetrated, the too close pressing semblance of reality, give a pain and an uneasiness which totally destroy all the delight which the words in the book convey, where the deed doing never presses upon us with the painful sense of presence; it rather seems to belong to history, —to something past and inevitable, if it has anything to do with time at all. The sublime images, the poetry alone, is that which is present to our minds in the reading.

So to see Lear acted, —to see an old man tottering about the stage with a walking-stick, turned out of doors by his daughters in a rainy night, has nothing in it but what is painful and disgusting. We want to take him into shelter and relieve him. That is all the feeling which the acting of Lear ever produced in me. But the Lear of Shakspeare cannot be acted. The contemptible machinery by which they mimic the storm which he goes out in, is not more inadequate to represent the horrors of the real elements, than any actor can be to represent Lear; they might more easily propose to personate the Satan of Milton upon a stage, or one of Michael Angelo's terrible figures. The greatness of Lear is not in corporal dimension, but in intellectual: the explosions of his passion are terrible as a volcano; they are storms turning up and disclosing to the bottom that sea, his mind, with all its vast riches. It is his mind which is laid bare. This case of flesh and blood seems too insignificant to be thought on; even as he himself neglects it. On the stage we see nothing but corporal infirmities and weakness, the impotence of rage; while we read it, we see not Lear, but we are Lear, —we are in his mind, we are sustained by a grandeur which baffles the malice of daughters and storms; in the aberrations of his reason, we discover a mighty irregular power of reasoning, immethodized from the ordinary purposes of life, but exerting its powers, as the wind blows where it listeth, at will upon the corruptions and abuses of mankind. What have looks, or tones, to do with that sublime identification of his age with that of the *heavens themselves*, when, in his reproaches to them for conniving at the injustice of his children, he reminds them that "they themselves are old? " What gesture shall we appropriate to this? What has the voice or the eye to do with such things? But the play is beyond all art, as the tamperings with it show; it is too hard and stony; it must have love-scenes, and a happy ending. It is not enough that Cordelia is a daughter, she must shine as a lover too. Tate has put his hook in the nostrils of this Leviathan, for Garrick and his followers, the showmen of the scene, to draw the mighty beast about more easily. A happy ending! —as if the living martyrdom that Lear had gone through, —the flaying of his feelings alive, did not make a fair dismissal from the stage of life the only decorous thing for him. If he is to live and be happy after, if he could sustain this world's burden after, why all this pudder and preparation, —why torment us with all this unnecessary sympathy? As if the childish pleasure of getting his gilt robes and sceptre again could tempt him to act over again his misused station, —as if, at his years and with his experience, anything was left but to die.

Lear is essentially impossible to be represented on a stage. But how many dramatic personages are there in Shakspeare, which though more tractable and feasible (if I may so speak) than Lear, yet from some circumstance, some adjunct to their character, are improper to be shown to our bodily eye! Othello, for instance. Nothing can be more soothing, more flattering to the nobler parts of our natures, than to read of a young Venetian lady of the highest extraction, through the force of love and from a sense of merit in him whom she loved, laying aside every consideration of kindred, and country, and color, and wedding with a *coal-black Moor*—(for such he is represented, in the imperfect state of knowledge respecting foreign countries in those days, compared with our own, or in compliance with popular notions, though the Moors are now well enough known to be by many shades less unworthy of a white woman's fancy)—it is the perfect triumph of virtue over accidents, of the imagination over the senses. She sees Othello's color in his mind. But upon the stage, when the imagination is no longer the ruling faculty, but we are left to our poor unassisted senses, I appeal to every one that has seen Othello played, whether he did not, on the contrary, sink Othello's mind in his color; whether he did not find something extremely revolting in the courtship and wedded caresses of Othello and Desdemona; and whether the actual sight of the thing did not overweigh all that beautiful compromise which we make in reading; —and the reason it should do so is obvious, because there is just so much reality presented to our senses as to give a perception of disagreement, with not enough of belief in the internal motives, —all that which is unseen, —to overpower and reconcile the first and obvious prejudices. [1] What we see upon a stage is body and bodily action; what we are conscious of in reading is almost exclusively the mind, and its movements; and this I think may sufficiently account for the very different sort of delight with which the same play so often affects us in the reading and the seeing.

[Footnote 1: The error of supposing that because Othello's color does not offend us in the reading, it should also not offend us in the seeing, is just such a fallacy as supposing that an Adam and Eve in a picture shall affect us just as they do in the poem. But in the poem we for a while have Paradisiacal senses given us, which vanish when we see a man and his wife without clothes in the picture. The painters themselves feel this, as is apparent by the awkward shifts they have recourse to, to make them look not quite naked; by a sort of prophetic anachronism, antedating the invention of fig-leaves. So in the reading of the play, we see with Desdemona's eyes: in the seeing of it, we are forced to look with our own. ]

It requires little reflection to perceive, that if those characters in Shakspeare which are within the precincts of nature, have yet something in them which appeals too exclusively to the imagination, to admit of their being made objects to the senses without suffering a change and a diminution, —that still stronger the objection must lie against representing another line of characters, which Shakspeare has introduced to give a wildness and a supernatural elevation to his scenes, as if to remove them still farther from that assimilation to common life in which their excellence is vulgarly supposed to consist. When we read the incantations of those terrible beings the Witches in Macbeth, though some of the ingredients of their hellish composition savor of the grotesque, yet is the effect upon us other than the most serious and appalling that can be imagined? Do we not feel spellbound as Macbeth was? Can any mirth accompany a sense of their presence? We might as well laugh under a consciousness of the principle of Evil himself being truly and really present with us. But attempt to bring these things on to a stage, and you turn them instantly into so many old women, that men and children are to laugh at. Contrary to the old saying, that "seeing is believing, " the sight actually destroys the faith; and the mirth in which we indulge at their expense, when we see these creatures upon a stage, seems to be a sort of indemnification which we make to ourselves for the terror which they put us in when reading made them an object of belief, —when we surrendered up our reason to the poet, as children to their nurses and their elders; and we laugh at our fears, as children, who thought they saw something in the dark, triumph when the bringing in of a candle discovers the vanity of their fears. For this exposure of supernatural agents upon a stage is truly bringing in a candle to expose their own delusiveness. It is the solitary taper and the book that generates a faith in these terrors: a ghost by chandelier light, and in good company, deceives no spectators, —a ghost that can be measured by the eye, and his human dimensions made out at leisure. The sight of a well-lighted house, and a well-dressed audience, shall arm the most nervous child against any apprehensions: as Tom Brown says of the impenetrable skin of Achilles with his impenetrable armor over it, "Bully Dawson would have fought the devil with such advantages. "

Much has been said, and deservedly, in reprobation of the vile mixture which Dryden has thrown into the Tempest: doubtless, without some such vicious alloy, the impure ears of that age would never have sat out to hear so much innocence of love as is contained in the sweet courtship of Ferdinand and Miranda. But is the tempest of Shakspeare at all a subject for stage-representation? It is one thing to read of an enchanter, and to believe the wondrous tale while we are reading it; but to have a conjurer brought before us in his conjuring gown, with his spirits about him, which none but himself and some hundred of favored spectators before the curtain are supposed to see, involves such a quantity of the *hateful incredible*, that all our reverence for the author cannot hinder us from perceiving such gross attempts upon the senses to be in the highest degree childish and inefficient. Spirits and fairies cannot be represented, they cannot even be painted, —they can only be believed. But the elaborate and anxious provision of scenery, which the luxury of the age demands, in these cases works a quite contrary effect to what is intended. That which in comedy, or plays of familiar life, adds so much to the life of the imitation, in plays which appeal to the higher faculties positively destroys the illusion which it is introduced to aid. A parlor or a drawing-room, —a library opening into a garden—a garden with an alcove in it, —a street, or the piazza of Covent Garden, does well enough in a scene; we are content to give as much credit to it as it demands; or rather, we think little about it, —it is little more than reading at the top of a page, "Scene, a garden; " we do not imagine ourselves there, but we readily admit the imitation of familiar objects. But to think by the help of painted trees and caverns, which we know to be painted, to transport our minds to Prospero, and his island and his lonely cell; [1] or by the aid of a fiddle dexterously thrown in, in an interval of speaking, to make us believe that we hear those supernatural noises of which the isle was full: the Orrery Lecturer at the Haymarket might as well hope, by his musical glasses cleverly stationed out of sight behind his apparatus, to make us believe that we do indeed hear the crystal spheres ring out that chime, which if it were to enwrap our fancy long, Milton thinks,

"Time would run back and fetch the age of gold,
And speckled Vanity
Would sicken soon and die,
And leprous Sin would melt from earthly mould;
Yea, Hell itself would pass away,
And leave its dolorous mansions to the peering day."

[Footnote 1: It will be said these things are done in pictures. But pictures and scenes are very different things. Painting is a world of itself; but in scene-painting there is the attempt to deceive; and there is the discordancy never to be got over, between painted scenes and real people. ]

The garden of Eden, with our first parents in it, is not more impossible to be shown on a stage, than the Enchanted isle, with its no less interesting and innocent first settlers.

The subject of Scenery is closely connected with that of the Dresses, which are so anxiously attended to on our stage. I remember the last time I saw Macbeth played, the discrepancy I felt at the changes of garment which he varied, the shiftings and reshiftings, like a Romish priest at mass. The luxury of stage-improvements, and the importunity of the public eye, require this. The coronation robe of the Scottish monarch was fairly a counterpart to that which our King wears when he goes to the Parliament house, just so full and cumbersome, and set out with ermine and pearls. And if things must be represented, I see not what to find fault with in this. But in reading, what robe are we conscious of? Some dim images of royalty—a crown and sceptre may float before our eyes, but who shall describe the fashion of it? Do we see in our mind's eye what Webb or any other robe-maker could pattern? This is the inevitable consequence of imitating everything, to make all things natural. Whereas the reading of a tragedy is a fine abstraction. It presents to the fancy just so much of external appearances as to make us feel that we are among flesh and blood, while by far the greater and better part of our imagination is employed upon the thoughts and internal machinery of the character. But in acting, scenery, dress, the most contemptible things, call upon us to judge of their naturalness.

Perhaps it would be no bad similitude, to liken the pleasure which we take in seeing one of these fine plays acted, compared with that quiet delight which we find in the reading of it, to the different feelings with which a reviewer, and a man that is not a reviewer, reads a fine poem. The accursed critical habit—the being called upon to judge and pronounce, must make it quite a different thing to the former. In seeing these plays acted, we are affected just as judges. When Hamlet compares the two pictures of Gertrude's first and second husband, who wants to see the pictures? But in the acting, a miniature must be lugged out; which we know not to be the picture, but only to show how finely a miniature may be represented. This showing of everything levels all things: it makes tricks, bows, and curtseys, of importance. Mrs. S. never got more fame by anything than by the manner in which she dismisses the guests in the banquet-scene in Macbeth: it is as much remembered as any of her thrilling tones or impressive looks. But does such a trifle as this enter into the imaginations of the readers of that wild and wonderful scene? Does not the mind dismiss the feasters as rapidly as it can? Does it care about the gracefulness of the doing it? But by acting, and judging of acting, all these non-essentials are raised into an importance, injurious to the main interest of the play.

I have confined my observations to the tragic parts of Shakspeare. It would be no very difficult task to extend the inquiry to his comedies; and to show why Falstaff, Shallow, Sir Hugh Evans, and the rest, are equally incompatible with stage-representation. The length to which this Essay has run will make it, I am afraid, sufficiently distasteful to the Amateurs of the Theatre, without going any deeper into the subject at present.

Essays

# CHARACTERS OF DRAMATIC WRITERS, CONTEMPORARY WITH SHAKSPEAKE.

\* \* \* \* \*

When I selected for publication, in 1808, "Specimens of English Dramatic Poets" who lived about the time of Shakspeare, the kind of extracts which I was anxious to give were not so much passages of wit and humor, though the old plays are rich in such, as scenes of passion, sometimes of the deepest quality, interesting situations, serious descriptions, that which is more nearly allied to poetry than to wit, and to tragic rather than to comic poetry. The plays which I made choice of were, with few exceptions, such as treat of human life and manners, rather than masques and Arcadian pastorals, with their train of abstractions, unimpassioned deities, passionate mortals—Claius, and Medorus, and Amintas, and Amaryllis. My leading design was to illustrate what may be called the moral sense of our ancestors. To show in what manner they felt when they placed themselves by the power of imagination in trying circumstances, in the conflicts of duty and passion, or the strife of contending duties; what sort of loves and enmities theirs were; how their griefs were tempered, and their full-swoln joys abated: how much of Shakspeare shines in the great men his contemporaries, and how far in his divine mind and manners he surpassed them and all mankind. I was also desirous to bring together some of the most admired scenes of Fletcher and Massinger, in the estimation of the world the only dramatic poets of that age entitled to be considered after Shakspeare, and, by exhibiting them in the same volume with the more impressive scenes of old Marlowe, Heywood, Tourneur, Webster, Ford, and others, to show what we had slighted, while beyond all proportion we had been crying up one or two favorite names. From the desultory criticisms which accompanied that publication, I have selected a few which I thought would best stand by themselves, as requiring least immediate reference to the play or passage by which they were suggested.

\* \* \* \* \*

## CHRISTOPHER MARLOWE.

*Lust's Dominion, or the Lascivious Queen.* —This tragedy is in King Cambyses' vein; rape, and murder, and superlatives; "huffing braggart puft lines, " such as the play-writers anterior to Shakspeare are full of, and Pistol but coldly imitates.

*Tamburlaine the Great, or the Scythian Shepherd.* —The lunes of Tamburlaine are perfect midsummer madness. Nebuchadnezzar's are mere modest pretensions compared with the thundering vaunts of this Scythian Shepherd. He comes in drawn by conquered kings, and reproaches these *pampered jades of Asia* that they can *draw but twenty miles a day*. Till I saw this passage with my own eyes, I never believed that it was anything more than a pleasant burlesque of mine Ancient's. But I can assure my readers that it is soberly set down in a play, which their ancestors took to be serious.

*Edward the Second.* —In a very different style from mighty Tamburlaine is the Tragedy of Edward the Second. The reluctant pangs of abdicating royalty in Edward furnished hints, which Shakspeare scarcely improved in his Richard the Second; and the death-scene of Marlowe's king moves pity and terror beyond any scene ancient or modern with which I am acquainted.

*The Rich Jew of Malta.* —Marlowe's Jew does not approach so near to Shakspeare's, as his Edward the Second does to Richard the Second. Barabas is a mere monster brought in with a large painted nose to please the rabble. He kills in sport, poisons whole nunneries, invents infernal machines. He is just such an exhibition as a century or two earlier might have been played before the Londoners "by the royal command, " when a general pillage and massacre of the Hebrews had been previously resolved on in the cabinet. It is curious to see a superstition wearing out. The idea of a Jew, which our pious ancestors contemplated with so much horror, has nothing in it now revolting. We have tamed the claws of the beast, and pared its nails, and now we take it to our arms, fondle it, write plays to flatter it; it is visited by princes, affects a taste, patronizes the arts, and is the only liberal and gentlemanlike thing in Christendom.

*Doctor Faustus.* —The growing horrors of Faustus's last scene are awfully marked by the hours and half hours as they expire, and bring him nearer and nearer to the exactment of his dire compact. It is indeed an agony and a fearful colluctation. Marlowe is said to have been tainted with atheistical positions, to have denied God and the Trinity. To such a genius the history of Faustus must have been delectable food: to wander in fields where curiosity is forbidden to go, to approach the dark gulf, near enough to look in, to be busied in speculations which are the rottenest part of the core of the fruit that fell from the tree of knowledge. [1] Barabas the Jew, and Faustus the conjurer, are offsprings of a mind which at least delighted to dally with interdicted subjects. They both talk a language which a believer would have been tender of putting into the mouth of a character though but in fiction. But the holiest minds have sometimes not thought it reprehensible to counterfeit impiety in the person of another, to bring Vice upon the stage speaking her own dialect; and, themselves being armed with an unction of self-confident impunity, have not scrupled to handle and touch that familiarly which would be death to others. Milton, in the person of Satan, has started speculations hardier than any which the feeble armory of the atheist ever furnished; and the precise, strait-laced Richardson has strengthened Vice, from the mouth of Lovelace, with entangling sophistries and abstruse pleas against her adversary Virtue, which Sedley, Villiers, and Rochester wanted depth of libertinism enough to have invented.

[Footnote 1: Error, entering into the world with Sin among us poor Adamites, may be said to spring from the tree of knowledge itself, and from the rotten kernels of that fatal apple. —*Howell's Letters.* ]

\* \* \* \* \*

## THOMAS DECKER.

*Old Fortunatus.* —The humor of a frantic lover in the scene where Orleans to his friend Galloway defends the passion with which himself, being a prisoner in the English king's court, is enamored to frenzy of the king's daughter Agripyna, is done to the life. Orleans is as passionate an inamorato as any which Shakspeare ever drew. He is just such another adept in Love's reasons. The sober people of the world are with him,

"A swarm of fools
Crowding together to be counted wise."

He talks "pure Biron and Romeo; " he is almost as poetical as they, quite as philosophical, only a little madder. After all, Love's sectaries are a reason unto themselves. We have gone retrograde to the noble heresy, since the days when Sidney proselyted our nation to this mixed health and disease: the kindliest symptom, yet the most alarming crisis, in the ticklish state of youth; the nourisher and the destroyer of hopeful wits; the mother of twin births, wisdom and folly, valor and weakness; the servitude above freedom; the gentle mind's religion; the liberal superstition.

*The Honest Whore.* —There is in the second part of this play, where Bellafront, a reclaimed harlot, recounts some of the miseries of her profession, a simple picture of honor and shame, contrasted without violence, and expressed without immodesty; which is worth all the *strong lines* against the harlot's profession, with which both parts of this play are offensively crowded. A satirist is always to be suspected, who, to make vice odious, dwells upon all its acts and minutest circumstances with a sort of relish and retrospective fondness. But so near are the boundaries of panegyric and invective, that a worn-out sinner is sometimes found to make the best declaimer against sin. The same high-seasoned descriptions, which in his unregenerate state served but to inflame his appetites, in his new province of a moralist will serve him, a little turned, to expose the enormity of those appetites in other men. When Cervantes, with such proficiency of fondness dwells upon the Don's library, who sees not that he has been a great reader of books of knight-errantry—perhaps was at some time of his life in danger of falling into those very extravagances which he ridiculed so happily in his hero!

\* \* \* \* \*

## JOHN MARSTON.

*Antonio and Mellida.* —The situation of Andrugio and Lucio, in the first part of this tragedy, —where Andrugio, Duke of Genoa, banished his country, with the loss of a son supposed drowned, is cast upon the territory of his mortal enemy the Duke of Venice, with no attendants but Lucio, an old nobleman, and a page—resembles that of Lear and Kent, in that king's distresses. Andrugio, like Lear, manifests a king-like impatience, a turbulent greatness, an affected resignation. The enemies which he enters lists to combat, "Despair and mighty Grief and sharp Impatience, " and the forces which he brings to vanquish them, "cornets of horse, " &c., are in the boldest style of allegory. They are such a "race of mourners" as the "infection of sorrows loud" in the intellect might beget on some "pregnant cloud" in the imagination. The prologue to the second part, for its passionate earnestness, and for the tragic note of preparation which it sounds, might have preceded one of those old tales of Thebes or Pelops' line, which Milton has so highly commended, as free from the common error of the poets in his day, of "intermixing comic stuff with tragic sadness and gravity, brought in without discretion corruptly to gratify the people. " It is as solemn a preparative as the "warning voice which he who saw the Apocalypse heard cry. "

*What You Will.* —*O I shall ne'er forget how he went cloath'd.* Act 1. Scene 1. —To judge of the liberality of these notions of dress, we must advert to the days of Gresham, and the consternation which a phenomenon habited like the merchant here described would have excited among the flat round caps, and cloth stockings upon 'Change, when those "original arguments or tokens of a citizen's vocation were in fashion, not more for thrift and usefulness than for distinction and grace. " The blank uniformity to which all professional distinctions in apparel have been long hastening is one instance of the decay of symbols among us, which, whether it has contributed or not to make us a more intellectual, has certainly made us a less imaginative people. Shakespeare knew the force of signs: a "malignant and turbaned Turk. " This "meal-cap miller, " says the author of God's Revenge against Murder, to express his indignation at an atrocious outrage committed by the miller Pierot upon the person of the fair Marieta.

\* \* \* \* \*

## AUTHOR UNKNOWN.

*The Merry Devil of Edmonton.* —The scene in this delightful comedy, in which Jerningham, "with the true feeling of a zealous friend, " touches the griefs of Mounchensey, seems written to make the reader happy. Few of our dramatists or novelists have attended enough to this. They torture and wound us abundantly. They are economists only in delight. Nothing can be finer, more gentlemanlike, and nobler, than the conversation and compliments of these young men. How delicious is Raymond Mounchensey's forgetting, in his fears, that Jerningham has a "Saint in Essex; " and how sweetly his friend reminds him! I wish it could be ascertained, which there is some grounds for believing, that Michael Drayton was the author of this piece. It would add a worthy appendage to the renown of that Panegyrist of my native Earth; who has gone over her soil, in his Polyolbion, with the fidelity of a herald, and the painful love of a son; who has not left a rivulet, so narrow that it may be stepped over, without honorable mention; and has animated hills and streams with life and passion beyond the dreams of old mythology.

\* \* \* \* \*

## THOMAS HEYWOOD.

*A Woman Killed with Kindness.* —Heywood is a sort of *prose* Shakspeare. His scenes are to the full as natural and affecting. But we miss *the poet*, that which in Shakspeare always appears out and above the surface of *the nature*. Heywood's characters, in this play, for instance, his country gentlemen, &c., are exactly what we see, but of the best kind of what we see in life. Shakspeare makes us believe, while we are among his lovely creations, that they are nothing but what we are familiar with, as in dreams new things seem old; but we awake, and sigh for the difference.

*The English Traveller.* —Heywood's preface to this play is interesting, as it shows the heroic indifference about the opinion of posterity, which some of these great writers seem to have felt. There is a magnanimity in authorship, as in everything else. His ambition seems to have been confined to the pleasure of hearing the players speak his lines while he lived. It does not appear that he ever contemplated the possibility of being read by after-ages. What a slender pittance of fame was motive sufficient to the production of such plays as the English Traveller, the Challenge for Beauty, and the Woman Killed with Kindness! Posterity is bound to take care that a writer loses nothing by such a noble modesty.

\* \* \* \* \*

## THOMAS MIDDLETON AND WILLIAM ROWLEY.

*A Fair Quarrel.* —The insipid levelling morality to which the modern stage is tied down, would not admit of such admirable passions as these scenes are filled with. A puritanical obtuseness of sentiment, a stupid infantile goodness, is creeping among us, instead of the vigorous passions, and virtues clad in flesh and blood, with which the old dramatists present us. Those noble and liberal casuists could discern in the differences, the quarrels, the animosities of men, a beauty and truth of moral feeling, no less than in the everlastingly inculcated duties of forgiveness and atonement. With us, all is hypocritical meekness. A reconciliation-scene, be the occasion never so absurd, never fails of applause. Our audiences come to the theatre to be complimented on their goodness. They compare notes with the amiable characters in the play, and find a wonderful sympathy of disposition between them. We have a common stock of dramatic morality, out of which a writer may be supplied without the trouble of copying it from originals within his own breast. To know the boundaries of honor, to be judiciously valiant, to have a temperance which shall beget a smoothness in the angry swellings of youth, to esteem life as nothing when the sacred reputation of a parent is to be defended, yet to shake and tremble under a pious cowardice when that ark of an honest confidence is found to be frail and tottering, to feel the true blows of a real disgrace blunting that sword which the imaginary strokes of a supposed false imputation had put so keen an edge upon but lately; to do, or to imagine this done, in a feigned story, asks something more of a moral sense, somewhat a greater delicacy of perception in questions of right and wrong, than goes to the writing of two or three hackneyed sentences about the laws of honor as opposed to the laws of the land, or a commonplace against duelling. Yet such things would stand a writer now-a-days in far better stead than Captain Agar and his conscientious honor; and he would be considered as a far better teacher of morality than old Rowley or Middleton, if they were living.

\* \* \* \* \*

## WILLIAM ROWLEY.

*A New Wonder; a Woman never Vext.* —The old play-writers are distinguished by an honest boldness of exhibition, —they show everything without being ashamed. If a reverse in fortune is to be exhibited, they fairly bring us to the prison-grate and the alms-basket. A poor man on our stage is always a gentleman; he may be known by a peculiar neatness of apparel, and by wearing black. Our delicacy, in fact, forbids the dramatizing of distress at all. It is never shown in its essential properties; it appears but as the adjunct of some virtue, as something which is to be relieved, from the approbation of which relief the spectators are to derive a certain soothing of self-referred satisfaction. We turn away from the real essences of things to hunt after their relative shadows, moral duties; whereas, if the truth of things were fairly represented, the relative duties might be safely trusted to themselves, and moral philosophy lose the name of a science.

# Essays

\* \* \* \* \*

## THOMAS MIDDLETON.

*The Witch.* —Though some resemblance may be traced between the charms in Macbeth and the incantations in this play, which is supposed to have preceded it, this coincidence will not detract much from the originality of Shakspeare. His witches are distinguished from the witches of Middleton by essential differences. These are creatures to whom man or woman, plotting some dire mischief, might resort for occasional consultation. Those originate deeds of blood, and begin bad impulses to men. From the moment that their eyes first meet with Macbeth's, he is spellbound. That meeting sways his destiny. He can never break the fascination. These witches can hurt the body; those have power over the soul. Hecate in Middleton has a son, a low buffoon: the hags of Shakspeare have neither child of their own, nor seem to be descended from any parent. They are foul anomalies, of whom we know not whence they are sprung, nor whether they have beginning or ending. As they are without human passions, so they seem to be without human relations. They come with thunder and lightning, and vanish to airy music. This is all we know of them. Except Hecate, they have no *names*; which heightens their mysteriousness. The names, and some of the properties which the other author has given to his hags, excite smiles. The Weïrd Sisters are serious things. Their presence cannot coexist with mirth. But in a lesser degree, the witches of Middleton are fine creations. Their power, too, is, in some measure, over the mind. They raise jars, jealousies, strifes, "like a thick scurf" over life.

\* \* \* \* \*

## WILLIAM ROWLEY, —THOMAS DECKER, —JOHN FORD, ETC.

*The Witch of Edmonton.* —Mother Sawyer, in this wild play, differs from the hags of both Middleton and Shakspeare. She is the plain, traditional old woman witch of our ancestors; poor, deformed, and ignorant; the terror of villages, herself amenable to a justice. That should he a hardy sheriff, with the power of the county at his heels, that would lay hands on the Weïrd Sisters. They are of another jurisdiction. But upon the common and received opinion, the author (or authors) have engrafted strong fancy. There is something frightfully earnest in her invocations to the Familiar.

# Essays

\* \* \* \* \*

## CYRIL TOURNEUR.

*The Revenger's Tragedy.* —The reality and life of the dialogue, in which Vindici and Hippolito first tempt their mother, and then threaten her with death for consenting to the dishonor of their sister, passes any scenical illusion I ever felt. I never read it but my ears tingle, and I feel a hot blush overspread my cheeks, as if I were presently about to proclaim such malefactions of myself, as the brothers here rebuke in their unnatural parent, in words more keen and dagger-like than those which Hamlet speaks to his mother. Such power has the passion of shame truly personated, not only to strike guilty creatures unto the soul, but to "appall" even those that are "free."

\* \* \* \* \*

## JOHN WEBSTER.

*The Duchess of Malfy.* —All the several parts of the dreadful apparatus with which the death of the Duchess is ushered in, the waxen images which counterfeit death, the wild masque of madmen, the tomb-maker, the bellman, the living person's dirge, the mortification by degrees, —are not more remote from the conceptions of ordinary vengeance, than the strange character of suffering which they seem to bring upon their victim is out of the imagination of ordinary poets. As they are not like inflictions of this life, so her language seems not of this world. She has lived among horrors till she is become "native and endowed unto that element." She speaks the dialect of despair; her tongue has a smatch of Tartarus and the souls in bale. To move a horror skilfully, to touch a soul to the quick, to lay upon fear as much as it can bear, to wean and weary a life till it is ready to drop, and then step in with mortal instruments to take its last forfeit: this only a Webster can do. Inferior geniuses may "upon horror's head horrors accumulate," but they cannot do this. They mistake quantity for quality; they "terrify babes with painted devils;" but they know not how a soul is to be moved. Their terrors want dignity, their affrightments are without decorum.

*The White Devil, or Vittoria Corombona.* —This White Devil of Italy sets off a bad cause so speciously, and pleads with such an innocence-resembling boldness, that we seem to see that matchless beauty of her face which inspires such gay confidence into her, and are ready to expect, when she has done her pleadings, that her very judges, her accusers, the grave ambassadors who sit as spectators, and all the court, will rise and make proffer to defend her, in spite of the utmost conviction of her guilt; as the Shepherds in Don Quixote make proffer to follow the beautiful Shepherdess Marcela, "without making any profit of her manifest resolution made there in their hearing. "

"So sweet and lovely does she make the shame,
Which, like a canker in the fragrant rose,
Does spot the beauty of her budding name!"

I never saw anything like the funeral dirge in this play for the death of Marcello, except the ditty which reminds Ferdinand of his drowned father in the Tempest. As that is of the water, watery; so this is of the earth, earthy. Both have that intenseness of feeling, which seems to resolve itself into the element which it contemplates.

In a note on the Spanish Tragedy in the Specimens, I have said that there is nothing in the undoubted plays of Jonson which would authorize us to suppose that he could have supplied the additions to Hieronymo. I suspected the agency of some more potent spirit. I thought that Webster might have furnished them. They seemed full of that wild, solemn, preternatural cast of grief which bewilders us in the Duchess of Malfy. On second consideration, I think this a hasty criticism. They are more like the overflowing griefs and talking distraction of Titus Andronicus. The sorrows of the Duchess set inward; if she talks, it is little more than soliloquy imitating conversation in a kind of bravery.

\* \* \* \* \*

## JOHN FORD.

*The Broken Heart.* —I do not know where to find, in any play, a catastrophe so grand, so solemn, and so surprising, as in this. This is indeed, according to Milton, to describe high passions and high actions. The fortitude of the Spartan boy, who let a beast gnaw out his bowels till he died, without expressing a groan, is a faint bodily image of this dilaceration of the spirit, and exenteration of the inmost mind, which Calantha, with a holy violence against her nature, keeps closely covered, till the last duties of a wife and a queen are fulfilled. Stories of martyrdom are but of chains and the stake; a little bodily suffering. These torments

> "On the purest spirits prey,
> As on entrails, joints, and limbs,
> With answerable pains, but more intense."

What a noble thing is the soul, in its strengths and in its weaknesses! Who would be less weak than Calantha? Who can be so strong? The expression of this transcendent scene almost bears us in imagination to Calvary and the Cross; and we seem to perceive some analogy between the scenical suffering which we are here contemplating and the real agonies of that final completion to which we dare no more than hint a reference. Ford was of the first order of poets. He sought for sublimity, not by parcels, in metaphors or visible images, but directly where she has her full residence, in the heart of man; in the actions and sufferings of the greatest minds. There is a grandeur of the soul, above mountains, seas, and the elements. Even in the poor perverted reason of Giovanni and Annabella, in the play[1] which stands at the head of the modern collection of the works of this author, we discern traces of that fiery particle, which, in the irregular starting from out the road of beaten action, discovers something of a right line even in obliquity, and shows hints of an improvable greatness in the lowest descents and degradations of our nature.

[Footnote: "'Tis Pity she's a Whore. "]

\* \* \* \* \*

## FULKE GREVILLE, LORD BROOKE.

*Alaham, Mustapha.* —The two tragedies of Lord Brooke, printed among his poems, might with more propriety have been termed political treatises than plays. Their author has strangely contrived to make passion, character, and interest, of the highest order, subservient to the expression of state dogmas and mysteries. He is in nine parts Machiavel and Tacitus, for one part Sophocles or Seneca. In this writer's estimate of the powers of the mind, the understanding must have held a most tyrannical preeminence. Whether we look into his plays or his most passionate love-poems, we shall find all frozen and made rigid with intellect. The finest movements of the human heart, the utmost grandeur of which the soul is capable, are essentially comprised in the actions and speeches of Cælica and Camena. Shakspeare, who seems to have had a peculiar delight in contemplating womanly perfection, whom for his many sweet images of female excellence all women are in an especial manner bound to love, has not raised the ideal of the female character higher than Lord Brooke, in these two women, has done. But it requires a study equivalent to the learning of a new language to understand their meaning when they speak. It is indeed hard to hit:

"Much like thy riddle, Samson, in one day
Or seven though one should musing sit."

It is as if a being of pure intellect should take upon him to express the emotions of our sensitive natures. There would be all knowledge, but sympathetic expressions would be wanting.

\* \* \* \* \*

## BEN JONSON.

*The Case is Altered*. —The passion for wealth has worn out much of its grossness in tract of time. Our ancestors certainly conceived of money as able to confer a distinct gratification in itself, not considered simply as a symbol of wealth. The old poets, when they introduce a miser, make him address his gold as his mistress; as something to be seen, felt, and hugged; as capable of satisfying two of the senses at least. The substitution of a thin, unsatisfying medium in the place of the good old tangible metal, has made avarice quite a Platonic affection in comparison with the seeing, touching, and handling pleasures of the old Chrysophilites. A bank-note can no more satisfy the touch of a true sensualist in this passion, than Creusa could return her husband's embrace in the shades. See the Cave of Mammon in Spenser; Barabas's contemplation of his wealth, in the Rich Jew of Malta; Luke's raptures in the City Madam; the idolatry and absolute gold-worship of the miser Jaques in this early comic production of Ben Jonson's. Above all, hear Guzman, in that excellent old translation of the Spanish Rogue, expatiate on the "ruddy cheeks of your golden ruddocks, your Spanish pistolets, your plump and full-faced Portuguese, and your clear-skinned pieces-of-eight of Castile, " which he and his fellows the beggars kept secret to themselves, and did privately enjoy in a plentiful manner. "For to have them to pay them away is not to enjoy them; to enjoy them is to have them lying by us; having no other need of them than to use them for the clearing of the eyesight, and the comforting of our senses. These we did carry about with us, sewing them in some patches of our doublets near unto the heart, and as close to the skin as we could handsomely quilt them in, holding them to be restorative. "

*Poetaster.* —This Roman play seems written to confute those enemies of Ben in his own days and ours, who have said that he made a pedantical use of his learning. He has here revived the whole Court of Augustus, by a learned spell. We are admitted to the society of the illustrious dead. Virgil, Horace, Ovid, Tibullus, converse in our own tongue more finely and poetically than they were used to express themselves in their native Latin. Nothing can be imagined more elegant, refined, and court-like, than the scenes between this Louis the Fourteenth of antiquity and his literati. The whole essence and secret of that kind of intercourse is contained therein. The economical liberality by which greatness, seeming to waive some part of its prerogative, takes care to lose none of the essentials; the prudential liberties of an inferior, which flatter by commanded boldness and soothe with complimentary sincerity; —these, and a thousand beautiful passages from his New Inn, his Cynthia's Revels, and from those numerous court-masques and entertainments, which he was in the daily habit of furnishing, might be adduced to show the poetical fancy and elegance of mind of the supposed rugged old bard.

*Alchemist.* —The judgment is perfectly overwhelmed by the torrent of images, words, and book-knowledge, with which Epicure Mammon (Act ii., Scene 2) confounds and stuns his incredulous hearer. They come pouring out like the successive falls of Nilus. They "doubly redouble strokes upon the foe. " Description outstrides proof. We are made to believe effects before we have testimony for their causes. If there is no one image which attains the height of the sublime, yet the confluence and assemblage of them all produces a result equal to the grandest poetry. The huge Xerxean army countervails against single Achilles. Epicure Mammon is the most determined offspring of its author. It has the whole "matter and copy of the father—eye, nose, lip, the trick of his frown. " It is just such a swaggerer as contemporaries have described old Ben to be. Meercraft, Bobadil, the Host of the New Inn, have all his image and superscription. But Mammon is arrogant pretension personified. Sir Samson Legend, in Love for Love, is such another lying, overbearing character, but he does not come up to Epicure Mammon. What a "towering bravery" there is in his sensuality! he affects no pleasure under a Sultan. It is as if "Egypt with Assyria strove in luxury."

\* \* \* \* \*

## GEORGE CHAPMAN.

*Bussy D'Ambois, Byron's Conspiracy, Byron's Tragedy*, &c. &c. — Webster has happily characterized the "full and heightened style" of Chapman, who, of all the English play-writers, perhaps approaches nearest to Shakspeare in the descriptive and didactic, in passages which are less purely dramatic. He could not go out of himself, as Shakspeare could shift at pleasure, to inform and animate other existences, but in himself he had an eye to perceive and a soul to embrace all forms and modes of being. He would have made a great epic poet, if indeed he has not abundantly shown himself to be one; for his Homer is not so properly a translation as the stories of Achilles and Ulysses rewritten. The earnestness and passion which he has put into every part of these poems would be incredible to a reader of mere modern translations. His almost Greek zeal for the glory of his heroes can only be paralleled by that fierce spirit of Hebrew bigotry, with which Milton, as if personating one of the zealots of the old law, clothed himself when he sat down to paint the acts of Samson against the uncircumcised. The great obstacle to Chapman's translations being read, is their unconquerable quaintness. He pours out in the same breath the most just and natural, and the most violent and crude expressions. He seems to grasp at whatever words come first to hand while the enthusiasm is upon him, as if all other must be inadequate to the divine meaning. But passion (the all in all in poetry) is everywhere present, raising the low, dignifying the mean, and putting sense into the absurd. He makes his readers glow, weep, tremble, take any affection which he pleases, be moved by words, or in spite of them, be disgusted, and overcome their disgust.

\* \* \* \* \*

## FRANCIS BEAUMONT. —JOHN FLETCHER.

*Maid's Tragedy.* —One characteristic of the excellent old poets is, their being able to bestow grace upon subjects which naturally do not seem susceptible of any. I will mention two instances. Zelmane in the Arcadia of Sidney, and Helena in the All's Well that Ends Well of Shakspeare. What can be more unpromising, at first sight, than the idea of a young man disguising himself in woman's attire, and passing himself off for a woman among women; and that for a long space of time? Yet Sir Philip has preserved so matchless a decorum, that neither does Pyrocles' manhood suffer any stain for the effeminacy of Zelmane, nor is the respect due to the princesses at all diminished when the deception comes to be known. In the sweetly-constituted mind of Sir Philip Sidney, it seems as if no ugly thought or unhandsome meditation could find a harbor. He turned all that he touched into images of honor and virtue. Helena in Shakspeare is a young woman seeking a man in marriage. The ordinary rules of courtship are reversed, the habitual feelings are crossed. Yet with such exquisite address this dangerous subject is handled, that Helena's forwardness loses her no honor; delicacy dispenses with its laws in her favor, and nature, in her single case, seems content to suffer a sweet violation. Aspatia, in the Maid's Tragedy, is a character equally difficult with Helena, of being managed with grace. She too is a slighted woman, refused by the man who had once engaged to marry her. Yet it is artfully contrived, that while we pity we respect her, and she descends without degradation. Such wonders true poetry and passion can do, to confer dignity upon subjects which do not seem capable of it. But Aspatia must not be compared at all points with Helena; she does not so absolutely predominate over her situation but she suffers some diminution, some abatement of the full lustre of the female character, which Helena never does. Her character has many degrees of sweetness, some of delicacy; but it has weakness, which, if we do not despise, we are sorry for. After all, Beaumont and Fletcher were but an inferior sort of Shakspeares and Sidneys.

*Philaster*. —The character of Bellario must have been extremely popular in its day. For many years after the date of Philaster's first exhibition on the stage, scarce a play can be found without one of these women-pages in it, following in the train of some pre-engaged lover, calling on the gods to bless her happy rival (his mistress), whom no doubt she secretly curses in her heart, giving rise to many pretty *equivoques* by the way on the confusion of sex, and either made happy at last by some surprising turn of fate, or dismissed with the joint pity of the lovers and the audience. Donne has a copy of verses to his mistress, dissuading her from a resolution, which she seems to have taken up from some of these scenical representations, of following him abroad as a page. It is so earnest, so weighty, so rich in poetry, in sense, in wit, and pathos, that it deserves to be read as a solemn close in future to all such sickly fancies as he there deprecates.

* * * * *

## JOHN FLETCHER.

*Thierry and Theodoret.* —The scene where Ordella offers her life a sacrifice, that the king of France may not be childless, I have always considered as the finest in all Fletcher, and Ordella to be the most perfect notion of the female heroic character, next to Calantha in the Broken Heart. She is a piece of sainted nature. Yet, noble as the whole passage is, it must be confessed that the manner of it, compared with Shakspeare's finest scenes, is faint and languid. Its motion is circular, not progressive. Each line revolves on itself in a sort of separate orbit. They do not join into one another like a running-hand. Fletcher's ideas moved slow; his versification, though sweet, is tedious, it stops at every turn; he lays line upon line, making up one after the other, adding image to image so deliberately, that we see their junctures. Shakspeare mingles everything, runs line into line, embarrasses sentences and metaphors; before one idea has burst its shell, another is hatched and clamorous for disclosure. Another striking difference between Fletcher and Shakspeare is the fondness of the former for unnatural and violent situations. He seems to have thought that nothing great could be produced in an ordinary way. The chief incidents in some of his most admired tragedies show this. [1] Shakspeare had nothing of this contortion in his mind, none of that craving after violent situations, and flights of strained and improbable virtue, which I think always betrays an imperfect moral sensibility. The wit of Fletcher is excellent, [2] like his serious scenes, but there is something strained and far-fetched in both. He is too mistrustful of Nature, he always goes a little on one side of her. —Shakspeare chose her without a reserve: and had riches, power, understanding, and length of days, with her for a dowry.

[Footnote 1: Wife for a Month, Cupid's Revenge, Double Marriage, &c. ]

[Footnote 2: Wit without Money, and his comedies generally. ]

*Faithful Shepherdess.* —If all the parts of this delightful pastoral had been in unison with its many innocent scenes and sweet lyric intermixtures, it had been a poem fit to vie with Comus or the Arcadia, to have been put into the hands of boys and virgins, to have made matter for young dreams, like the loves of Hermia and Lysander. But a spot is on the face of this Diana. Nothing short of infatuation could have driven Fletcher upon mixing with this "blessedness" such an ugly deformity as Chloe, the wanton shepherdess! If Chloe was meant to set off Clorin by contrast, Fletcher should have known that such weeds by juxtaposition do not set off, but kill sweet flowers.

\* \* \* \* \*

## PHILIP MASSINGER. —THOMAS DECKER.

*The Virgin Martyr.* —This play has some beauties of so very high an order, that with all my respect for Massinger, I do not think he had poetical enthusiasm capable of rising up to them. His associate Decker who wrote Old Fortunatus, had poetry enough for anything. The very impurities which obtrude themselves among the sweet pieties of this play, like Satan among the Sons of Heaven, have a strength of contrast, a raciness, and a glow, in them, which are beyond Massinger. They are to the religion of the rest what Caliban is to Miranda.

\* \* \* \* \*

## PHILIP MASSINGER. —THOMAS MIDDLETON. —WILLIAM ROWLEY.

*Old Law.* —There is an exquisiteness of moral sensibility, making one's eyes to gush out tears of delight, and a poetical strangeness in the circumstances of this sweet tragicomedy, which are unlike anything in the dramas which Massinger wrote alone. The pathos is of a subtler edge. Middleton and Rowley, who assisted in it, had both of them finer geniuses than their associate.

\* \* \* \* \*

## JAMES SHIRLEY

Claims a place amongst the worthies of this period, not so much for any transcendent talent in himself, as that he was the last of a great race, all of whom spoke nearly the same language, and had a set of moral feelings and notions in common. A new language, and quite a new turn of tragic and comic interest, came in with the Restoration.

Essays

## SPECIMENS FROM THE WRITINGS OF FULLER,

## THE CHURCH HISTORIAN.

The writings of Fuller are usually designated by the title of quaint, and with sufficient reason; for such was his natural bias to conceits, that I doubt not upon most occasions it would have been going out of his way to have expressed himself out of them. But his wit is not always a *lumen siccum,* a dry faculty of surprising; on the contrary, his conceits are oftentimes deeply steeped in human feeling and passion. Above all, his way of telling a story, for its eager liveliness, and the perpetual running commentary of the narrator happily blended with the narration, is perhaps unequalled.

As his works are now scarcely perused but by antiquaries, I thought it might not be unacceptable to my readers to present them with some specimens of his manner, in single thoughts and phrases; and in some few passages of greater length, chiefly of a narrative description. I shall arrange them as I casually find them in my book of extracts, without being solicitous to specify the particular work from which they are taken.

*Pyramids.* —"The Pyramids themselves, doting with age, have forgotten the names of their founders."

*Virtue in a Short Person.* —"His soul had but a short diocese to visit, and therefore might the better attend the effectual informing thereof."

*Intellect in a very Tall One.* —"Ofttimes such who are built four stories high, are observed to have little in their cockloft."

*Naturals.* —"Their heads sometimes so little, that there is no room for wit; sometimes so long, that there is no wit for so much room."

*Negroes.* —"The image of God cut in ebony."

*School-Divinity.* —"At the first it will be as welcome to thee as a prison, and their very solutions will seem knots unto thee."

*Mr. Perkins the Divine.* —"He had a capacious head, with angles winding and roomy enough to lodge all controversial intricacies."

*The same.* —"He would pronounce the word *Damn* with such an emphasis as left a doleful echo in his auditors' ears a good while after."

*Judges in Capital Cases.* —"O let him take heed how he strikes that hath a dead hand."

*Memory.* —"Philosophers place it in the rear of the head, and it seems the mine of memory lies there, because there men naturally dig for it, scratching it when they are at a loss."

*Fancy.* —"It is the most boundless and restless faculty of the soul; for while the Understanding and the Will are kept, as it were, *in libera custodia* to their objects of *verum et bonum*, the Fancy is free from all engagements: it digs without spade, sails without ship, flies without wings, builds without charges, fights without bloodshed; in a moment striding from the centre to the circumference of the world; by a kind of omnipotency creating and annihilating things in an instant; and things divorced in Nature are married in Fancy as in a lawless place."

*Infants.* —"Some, admiring what motives to mirth infants meet with in their silent and solitary smiles, have resolved, how truly I know not, that then they converse with angels; as indeed such cannot among mortals find any fitter companions."

*Music.* —"Such is the sociableness of music, it conforms itself to all companies both in mirth and mourning; complying to improve that passion with which it finds the auditors most affected. In a word, it is an invention which might have beseemed a son of Seth to have been the father thereof: though better it was that Cain's great-grandchild should have the credit first to find it, than the world the unhappiness longer to have wanted it."

*St. Monica.* —"Drawing near her death, she sent most pious thoughts as harbingers to heaven, and her soul saw a glimpse of happiness through the chinks of her sickness-broken body."[1]

[Footnote 1:

"The soul's dark cottage, batter'd and decay'd, Lets in new lights through chinks which time has made." WALLER. ]

# Essays

*Mortality.* —"To smell to a turf of fresh earth is wholesome for the body, no less are thoughts of mortality cordial to the soul."

*Virgin.* —"No lordling husband shall at the same time command her presence and distance; to be always near in constant attendance, and always to stand aloof in awful observance."

*Elder Brother.* —"Is one who made haste to come into the world to bring his parents the first news of male posterity, and is well rewarded for his tidings."

*Bishop Fletcher.* —"His pride was rather on him than in him, as only gait and gesture deep, not sinking to his heart, though causelessly condemned for a proud man, as who was a *good hypocrite*, and far more humble than he appeared."

*Masters of Colleges.* —"A little allay of dulness in a Master of a College makes him fitter to manage secular affairs."

*The Good Yeoman.* —"Is a gentleman in ore, whom the next age may see refined."

*Good Parent.* —"For his love, therein like a well-drawn picture, he eyes all his children alike."

*Deformity in Children.* —"This partiality is tyranny, when parents despise those that are deformed; *enough to break those whom God had bowed before.*"

*Good Master.* —"In correcting his servant he becomes not a slave to his own passion. Not cruelly making new *indentures* of the flesh of his apprentice. He is tender of his servant in sickness and age. If crippled in his service, his house is his hospital. Yet how many throw away those dry bones, out of the which themselves have sucked the marrow!"

*Good Widow.* —"If she can speak but little good of him [her dead husband] she speaks but little of him. So handsomely folding up her discourse, that his virtues are shown outwards, and his vices wrapt up in silence; as counting it barbarism to throw dirt on his memory, who hath mould cast on his body."

*Horses.* —"These are men's wings, wherewith they make such speed. A generous creature a horse is, sensible in some sort of honor; and made most handsome by that which deforms men most—pride. "

*Martyrdom.* —"Heart of oak hath sometimes warped a little in the scorching heat of persecution. Their want of true courage herein cannot be excused. Yet many censure them for surrendering up their forts after a long siege, who would have yielded up their own at the first summons. —Oh! there is more required to make one valiant, than to call Cranmer or Jewel coward; as if the fire in Smithfield had been no hotter than what is painted in the Book of Martyrs. "

*Text of St. Paul.* —"St. Paul saith, Let not the sun go down on your wrath, to carry news to the antipodes in another world of thy revengeful nature. Yet let us take the Apostle's meaning rather than his words, with all possible speed to depose our passion; not understanding him so literally, that we may take leave to be angry till sunset: then might our wrath lengthen with the days; and men in Greenland, where the day lasts above a quarter of a year, have plentiful scope for revenge. "[1]

[Footnote 1: This whimsical prevention of a consequence which no one would have thought of deducing, —setting up an absurdum on purpose to hunt it down, —placing guards as it were at the very outposts of possibility, —gravely giving out laws to insanity and prescribing moral fences to distempered intellects, could never have entered into a head less entertainingly constructed than that of Fuller or Sir Thomas Browne, the very air of whose style the conclusion of this passage most aptly imitates. ]

*Bishop Brownrig.* —"He carried learning enough *in numerato* about him in his pockets for any discourse, and had much more at home in his chests for any serious dispute. "

*Modest Want.* —"Those that with diligence fight against poverty, though neither conquer till death makes it a drawn battle, expect not but prevent their craving of thee: for God forbid the heavens should never rain, till the earth first opens her mouth; seeing *some grounds will sooner burn than chap.* "

*Death-bed Temptations.* —"The devil is most busy on the last day of his term; and a tenant to be ousted cares not what mischief he doth. "

*Conversation.* —"Seeing we are civilized Englishmen, let us not be naked savages in our talk. "

*Wounded Soldier.* —"Halting is the stateliest march of a soldier; and 'tis a brave sight to see the flesh of an ancient as torn as his colors. "

*Wat Tyler.* —"A *misogrammatist*; if a good Greek word may be given to so barbarous a rebel. "

*Heralds.* —"Heralds new mould men's names—taking from them, adding to them, melting out all the liquid letters, torturing mutes to make them speak, and making vowels dumb, —to bring it to a fallacious *homonomy* at the last, that their names may be the same with those noble houses they pretend to. "

*Antiquarian Diligence.* —"It is most worthy observation, with what diligence he [Camden] inquired after ancient places, making hue and cry after many a city which was run away, and by certain marks and tokens pursuing to find it; as by the situation on the Roman highways, by just distance from other ancient cities, by some affinity of name, by tradition of the inhabitants, by Roman coins digged up, and by some appearance of ruins. A broken urn is a whole evidence; or an old gate still surviving, out of which the city is run out. Besides, commonly some new spruce town not far off is grown out of the ashes thereof, which yet hath so much natural affection as dutifully to own those reverend ruins for her mother. "

*Henry de Essex.* —"He is too well known in our English Chronicles, being Baron of Raleigh, in Essex, and Hereditary Standard Bearer of England. It happened in the reign of this king [Henry II. ] there was a fierce battle fought in Flintshire, at Coleshall, between the English and Welsh, wherein this Henry de Essex *animum et signum simul abjecit*, betwixt traitor and coward, cast away both his courage and banner together, occasioning a great overthrow of English. But he that had the baseness to do, had the boldness to deny the doing of so foul a fact; until he was challenged in combat by Robert de Momford, a knight, eye-witness thereof, and by him overcome in a duel. Whereupon his large inheritance was confiscated to the king, and he himself, *partly thrust, partly going into a convent, hid his head in a cowl, under which, betwixt shame and sanctity, he blushed out the remainder of his life.* "[1]—*Worthies*, article *Bedfordshire*.

[Footnote 1: The fine imagination of Fuller has done what might have been pronounced impossible. It has given an interest, and a holy character to coward infamy. Nothing can be more beautiful than the concluding account of the last days, and expiatory retirement, of poor Henry de Essex. The address with which the whole of this little story is told is most consummate; the charm of it seems to consist in a perpetual balance of antithesis not too violently opposed, and the consequent activity of mind in which the reader is kept: —"Betwixt traitor and coward"—"baseness to do, boldness to deny"—"partly thrust, partly going, into a convent"—"betwixt shame and sanctity. " The reader by this artifice is taken into a kind of partnership with the writer, —his judgment is exercised in settling the preponderance, —he feels as if he were consulted as to the issue. But the modern historian flings at once the dead weight of his own judgment into the scale, and settles the matter. ]

*Sir Edward Harwood, Knt.* —"I have read of a bird, which hath a face like, and yet will prey upon, a man: who coming to the water to drink, and finding there by reflection, that he had killed one like himself, pineth away by degrees, and never afterwards enjoyeth itself. [1] Such is in some sort the condition of Sir Edward. This accident, that he had killed one in a private quarrel, put a period to his carnal mirth, and was a covering to his eyes all the days of his life. No possible provocations could afterwards tempt him to a duel; and no wonder that one's conscience loathed that whereof he had surfeited. He refused all challenges with more honor than others accepted them; it being well known that he would set his foot as far in the face of his enemy as any man alive. "—*Worthies*, article *Lincolnshire*.

[Footnote 1: I do not know where Fuller read of this bird; but a more awful and affecting story, and moralizing of a story, in Natural History, or rather in that Fabulous Natural History where poets and mythologists found the Phoenix and the Unicorn and "other strange fowl, " is nowhere extant. It is a fable which Sir Thomas Browne, if he had heard of it, would have exploded among his Vulgar Errors; but the delight which he would have taken in the discussing of its probabilities, would have shown that the *truth of the fact*, though the avowed object of his search was not so much the motive which put him upon the investigation, as those hidden affinities and poetical analogies, —those *essential verities* in the application of strange fable, which made him linger with such reluctant delay among the last fading lights of popular tradition; and not seldom to conjure up a superstition, that had been long extinct, from its dusty grave, to inter it himself with greater ceremonies and solemnities of burial. ]

*Decayed Gentry.* —"It happened in the reign of King James, when Henry Earl of Huntingdon was Lieutenant of Leicestershire, that a laborer's son in that country was pressed into the wars; as I take it, to go over with Count Mansfield. The old man at Leicester requested his son might be discharged, as being the only staff of his age, who by his industry maintained him and his mother. The Earl demanded his name, which the man for a long time was loath to tell (as suspecting it a fault for so poor a man to confess the truth); at last he told his name was Hastings. 'Cousin Hastings, ' said the Earl, 'we cannot all be top branches of the tree, though we all spring from the same root; your son, my kinsman, shall not be pressed.' So good was the meeting of modesty in a poor, with courtesy in an honorable person, and gentry I believe in both. And I have reason to believe, that some who justly own the surnames and blood of Bohuns, Mortimers, and Plantagenets (though ignorant of their own extractions), are hid in the heap of common people, where they find that under a thatched cottage which some of their ancestors could not enjoy in a leaded castle—contentment, with quiet and security."—*Worthies*, article *Of Shire-Reeves or Shiriffes*.

*Tenderness of Conscience in a Tradesman.* —"Thomas Curson, born in Allhallows, Lombard Street, armorer, dwelt without Bishopsgate. It happened that a stage-player borrowed a rusty musket, which had lain long leger in his shop: now though his part were comical, he therewith acted an unexpected tragedy, killing one of the standers-by, the gun casually going off on the stage, which he suspected not to be charged. O the difference of divers men in the tenderness of their consciences! some are scarce touched with a wound, whilst others are wounded with a touch therein. This poor armorer was highly afflicted therewith, though done against his will, yea, without his knowledge, in his absence, by another, out of mere chance. Hereupon he resolved to give all his estate to pious uses: no sooner had he gotten a round sum, but presently he posted with it in his apron to the Court of Aldermen, and was in pain till by their direction he had settled it for the relief of poor in his own and other parishes, and disposed of some hundreds of pounds accordingly, as I am credibly informed by the then churchwardens of the said parish. Thus, as he conceived himself casually (though at a great distance) to have occasioned the death of one, he was the immediate and direct cause of giving a comfortable living to many. "

*Burning of Wickliffe's Body by Order of the Council of Constance.* — "Hitherto [A. D. 1428] the corpse of John Wickliffe had quietly slept in his grave about forty-one years after his death, till his body was reduced to bones, and his bones almost to dust. For though the earth in the chancel of Lutterworth, in Leicestershire, where he was interred, hath not so quick a digestion with the earth of Aceldama, to consume flesh in twenty-four hours, yet such the appetite thereof, and all other English graves, to leave small reversions of a body after so many years. But now such the spleen of the Council of Constance, as they not only cursed his memory as dying an obstinate heretic, but ordered that his bones (with this charitable caution, —if it may be discerned from the bodies of other faithful people) be taken out of the ground, and thrown far off from any Christian burial. In obedience hereunto, Richard Fleming, Bishop of Lincoln, Diocesan of Lutterworth, sent his officers (vultures with a quick sight, scent, at a dead carcass) to ungrave him. Accordingly to Lutterworth they come, Sumner, Commissary, Official, Chancellor, Proctors, Doctors, and their servants, (so that the remnant of the body would not hold out a bone amongst so many hands, ) take what was left out of the grave, and burnt them to ashes, and cast them into Swift, a neighboring brook, running hard by. *Thus this brook has conveyed his ashes into Avon, Avon into Severn, Severn into the narrow seas, they into the main ocean; and thus the ashes of Wickliffe are the emblem of his doctrine, which now is dispersed all the world over.* "[1]—Church History.

[Footnote 1: The concluding period of this most lively narrative I will not call a conceit: it is one of the grandest conceptions I ever met with. One feels the ashes of Wickliffe gliding away out of the reach of the Sumners, Commissaries, Officials, Proctors, Doctors, and all the puddering rout of executioners of the impotent rage of the baffled Council: from Swift into Avon, from Avon into Severn, from Severn into the narrow seas, from the narrow seas into the main ocean, where they become the emblem of his doctrine, "dispersed all the world over. " Hamlet's tracing the body of Cæsar to the clay that stops a beer-barrel is a no less curious pursuit of "ruined mortality; " but it is in an inverse ratio to this: it degrades and saddens us, for one part of our nature at least; but this expands the whole of our nature, and gives to the body a sort of ubiquity, —a diffusion as far as the actions of its partner can have reach or influence.

I have seen this passage smiled at, and set down as a quaint conceit of old Fuller. But what is not a conceit to those who read it in a temper different from that in which the writer composed it? The most pathetic parts of poetry to cold tempers seem and are nonsense, as divinity was to the Greeks foolishness. When Richard II., meditating on his own utter annihilation as to royalty, cries out,

"O that I were a mockery king of snow, To melt before the sun of Bolingbroke, "

if we had been going on pace for pace with the passion before, this sudden conversion of a strong-felt metaphor into something to be actually realized in nature, like that of Jeremiah, "Oh! that my head were waters, and mine eyes a fountain of tears, " is strictly and strikingly natural; but come unprepared upon it, and it is a conceit: and so is a "head" turned into "waters."]

Essays

## ON THE

## GENIUS AND CHARACTER OF HOGARTH;

## WITH SOME REMARKS ON A PASSAGE IN THE WRITINGS OF THE LATE MR. BARRY.

\* \* \* \* \*

One of the earliest and noblest enjoyments I had when a boy, was in the contemplation of those capital prints by Hogarth, the *Harlot's* and *Rake's Progresses*, which, along with some others, hung upon the walls of a great hall in an old-fashioned house in — —shire, and seemed the solitary tenants (with myself) of that antiquated and life-deserted apartment.

Recollection of the manner in which those prints used to affect me has often made me wonder, when I have heard Hogarth described as a mere comic painter, as one of those whose chief ambition was to *raise a laugh*. To deny that there are throughout the prints which I have mentioned circumstances introduced of a laughable tendency, would be to run counter to the common notions of mankind; but to suppose that in their *ruling character* they appeal chiefly to the risible faculty, and not first and foremost to the very heart of man, its best and most serious feelings, would be to mistake no less grossly their aim and purpose. A set of severer Satires (for they are not so much Comedies, which they have been likened to, as they are strong and masculine Satires) less mingled with anything of mere fun, were never written upon paper, or graven upon copper. They resemble Juvenal, or the satiric touches in Timon of Athens.

I was pleased with the reply of a gentleman, who being asked which book he esteemed most in his library, answered, —"Shakspeare: " being asked which he esteemed next best, replied, "Hogarth. " His graphic representations are indeed books: they have the teeming, fruitful, suggestive meaning of *words*. Other pictures we look at, — his prints we read.

In pursuance of this parallel, I have sometimes entertained myself with comparing the *Timon of Athens* of Shakespeare (which I have just mentioned) and Hogarth's *Rake's Progress* together. The story, the moral, in both is nearly the same. The wild course of riot and extravagance, ending in the one with driving the Prodigal from the society of men into the solitude of the deserts, and in the other with conducting the Rake through his several stages of dissipation into the still more complete desolations of the mad-house, in the play and in the picture, are described with almost equal force and nature. The levee of the Rake, which forms the subject of the second plate in the series, is almost a transcript of Timon's levee in the opening scene of that play. We find a dedicating poet, and other similar characters, in both.

The concluding scene in the *Rake's Progress* is perhaps superior to the last scenes of *Timon*. If we seek for something of kindred excellence in poetry, it must be in the scenes of Lear's beginning madness, where the King and the Fool and the Tom-o'-Bedlam conspire to produce such a medley of mirth checked by misery, and misery rebuked by mirth; where the society of those "strange bedfellows" which misfortunes have brought Lear acquainted with, so finely sets forth the destitute state of the monarch; while the lunatic bans of the one, and the disjointed sayings and wild but pregnant allusions of the other, so wonderfully sympathize with that confusion, which they seem to assist in the production of, in the senses of that "child-changed father. "

In the scene in Bedlam, which terminates the *Rake's Progress*, we find the same assortment of the ludicrous with the terrible. Here is desperate madness, the overturning of originally strong thinking faculties, at which we shudder, as we contemplate the duration and pressure of affliction which it must have asked to destroy such a building; —and here is the gradual hurtless lapse into idiocy, of faculties, which at their best of times never having been strong, we look upon the consummation of their decay with no more of pity than is consistent with a smile. The mad tailor, the poor driveller that has gone out of his wits (and truly he appears to have had no great journey to go to get past their confines) for the love of *Charming Betty Careless*, —. these half-laughable, scarce-pitiable objects, take off from the horror which the principal figure would of itself raise, at the same time that they assist the feeling of the scene by contributing to the general notion of its subject: —

"Madness, thou chaos of the brain,
What art, that pleasure giv'st and pain?
Tyranny of Fancy's reign!
Mechanic Fancy, that can build

Vast labyrinths and mazes wild,
With rule disjointed, shapeless measure,
Fill'd with horror, fill'd with pleasure!
Shapes of horror, that would even
Cast doubts of mercy upon heaven;
Shapes of pleasure, that but seen,
Would split the shaking sides of Spleen."[1]

[Footnote 1: Lines inscribed under the plate]

Is it carrying the spirit of comparison to excess to remark, that in the poor kneeling weeping female who accompanies her seducer in his sad decay, there is something analogous to Kent, or Caius, as he delights rather to be called, in *Lear*, —the noblest pattern of virtue which even Shakspeare has conceived, —who follows his royal master in banishment, that had pronounced *his* banishment, and forgetful at once of his wrongs and dignities, taking on himself the disguise of a menial, retains his fidelity to the figure, his loyalty to the carcass, the shadow, the shell, and empty husk of Lear?

In the perusal of a book, or of a picture, much of the impression which we receive depends upon the habit of mind which we bring with us to such perusal. The same circumstance may make one person laugh, which shall render another very serious; or in the same person the first impression may be corrected by after-thought. The misemployed incongruous characters at the *Harlot's Funeral*, on a superficial inspection, provoke to laughter; but when we have sacrificed the first emotion to levity, a very different frame of mind succeeds, or the painter has lost half his purpose. I never look at that wonderful assemblage of depraved beings, who, without a grain of reverence or pity in their perverted minds, are performing the sacred exteriors of duty to the relics of their departed partner in folly, but I am as much moved to sympathy from the very want of it in them, as I should be by the finest representation of a virtuous death-bed surrounded by real mourners, pious children, weeping friends, — perhaps more by the very contrast. What reflections does it not awake, of the dreadful heartless state in which the creature (a female too) must have lived, who in death wants the accompaniment of one genuine tear. That wretch who is removing the lid of the coffin to gaze upon the corpse with a face which indicates a perfect negation of all goodness or womanhood—the hypocrite parson and his demure partner—all the fiendish group—to a thoughtful mind present a moral emblem more affecting than if the poor friendless carcass had been depicted as thrown out to the woods, where wolves had assisted at its obsequies, itself furnishing forth its own funeral banquet.

It is easy to laugh at such incongruities as are met together in this picture, —incongruous objects being of the very essence of laughter, —but surely the laugh is far different in its kind from that thoughtless species to which we are moved by mere farce and grotesque. We laugh when Ferdinand Count Fathom, at the first sight of the white cliffs of Britain, feels his heart yearn with filial fondness towards the land of his progenitors, which he is coming to fleece and plunder, —we smile at the exquisite irony of the passage, —but if we are not led on by such passages to some more salutary feeling than laughter, we are very negligent perusers of them in book or picture.

It is the fashion with those who cry up the great Historical School in this country, at the head of which Sir Joshua Reynolds is placed, to exclude Hogarth from that school, as an artist of an inferior and vulgar class. Those persons seem to me to confound the painting of subjects in common or vulgar life with the being a vulgar artist. The quantity of thought which Hogarth crowds into every picture would alone *unvulgarize* every subject which he might choose. Let us take the lowest of his subjects, the print called *Gin Lane*. Here is plenty of poverty, and low stuff to disgust upon a superficial view; and accordingly a cold spectator feels himself immediately disgusted and repelled. I have seen many turn away from it, not being able to bear it. The same persons would perhaps have looked with great complacency upon Poussin's celebrated picture of the *Plague at Athens*[1] Disease and Death and bewildering Terror, in *Athenian garments*, are endurable, and come, as the delicate critics express it, within the "limits of pleasurable sensation. " But the scenes of their own St. Giles's, delineated by their own countryman, are too shocking to think of. Yet if we could abstract our minds from the fascinating colors of the picture, and forget the coarse execution (in some respects) of the print, intended as it was to be a cheap plate, accessible to the poorer sort of people, for whose instruction it was done, I think we could have no hesitation in conferring the palm of superior genius upon Hogarth, comparing this work of his with Poussin's picture. There is more of imagination in it—that power which draws all things to one, —which makes things animate and inanimate, beings with their attributes, subjects, and their accessories, take one color and serve to one effect. Everything in the print, to use a vulgar expression, *tells*. Every part is full of "strange images of death. " It is perfectly amazing and astounding to look at. Not only the two prominent figures, the woman and the half-dead man, which are as terrible as anything which Michael Angelo ever drew, but everything else in the print, contributes to bewilder and stupefy, —the very houses, as I heard a friend of mine express it, tumbling all about in various directions, seem drunk—seem absolutely reeling from the effect of that diabolical spirit of frenzy which goes forth over the whole composition. To show the poetical and almost prophetical conception in the artist, one little circumstance may serve. Not content with the dying and dead figures, which he has strewed in profusion over the proper scene of the action, he shows you what (of a kindred nature) is passing beyond it. Close by the shell, in which, by direction of the parish beadle, a man is depositing his wife, is an old wall, which, partaking of the universal decay around it, is tumbling to pieces. Through a gap in this wall are seen three figures, which appear to make a part in some funeral procession which is passing by on the other side of the wall, out of the sphere of the composition. This extending of the interest beyond the bounds of the subject could only have been conceived by a great genius. Shakspeare, in his description of the painting of the Trojan War, in his *Tarquin and Lucrece*, has introduced a similar device, where the painter made a part stand for the whole: —

"For much imaginary work was there,
Conceit deceitful, so compact, so kind,
That for Achilles' image stood his spear,
Grip'd in an armed hand; himself behind
Was left unseen, save to the eye of mind:
A hand, a foot, a face, a leg, a head,
Stood for the whole to be imagined."

[Footnote 1: At the late Mr. Hope's, in Cavendish Square]

This he well calls *imaginary work*, where the spectator must meet the artist in his conceptions half way; and it is peculiar to the confidence of high genius alone to trust so much to spectators or readers. Lesser artists show everything distinct and full, as they require an object to be made out to themselves before they can comprehend it.

When I think of the power displayed in this (I will not hesitate to say) sublime print, it seems to me the extreme narrowness of system alone, and of that rage for classification, by which, in matters of taste at least, we are perpetually perplexing, instead of arranging, our ideas, that would make us concede to the work of Poussin above mentioned, and deny to this of Hogarth, the name of a grand serious composition.

We are forever deceiving ourselves with names and theories. We call one man a great historical painter, because he has taken for his subjects kings or great men, or transactions over which time has thrown a grandeur. We term another the painter of common life, and set him down in our minds for an artist of an inferior class, without reflecting whether the quantity of thought shown by the latter may not much more than level the distinction which their mere choice of subjects may seem to place between them; or whether, in fact, from that very common life a great artist may not extract as deep an interest as another man from that which we are pleased to call history.

I entertain the highest respect for the talents and virtues of Reynolds, but I do not like that his reputation should overshadow and stifle the merits of such a man as Hogarth, nor that to mere names and classifications we should be content to sacrifice one of the greatest ornaments of England.

I would ask the most enthusiastic admirer of Reynolds, whether in the countenances of his *Staring* and *Grinning Despair*, which he has given us for the faces of Ugolino and dying Beaufort, there be anything comparable to the expression which Hogarth has put into the face of his broken-down rake in the last plate but one of the *Rake's Progress*, [1] where a letter from the manager is brought to him to say that his play "will not do? " Here all is easy, natural, undistorted, but withal what a mass of woe is here accumulated! — the long history of a misspent life is compressed into the countenance as plainly as the series of plates before had told it; here is no attempt at Gorgonian looks, which are to freeze the beholder — no grinning at the antique bedposts — no face-making, or consciousness of the presence of spectators in or out of the picture, but grief kept to a man's self, a face retiring from notice with the shame which great anguish sometimes brings with it, —a final leave taken of hope, —the coming on of vacancy and stupefaction, —a beginning alienation of mind looking like tranquillity. Here is matter for the mind of the beholder to feed on for the hour together, — matter to feed and fertilize the mind. It is too real to admit one thought about the power of the artist who did it. When we compare the expression in subjects which so fairly admit of comparison, and find the superiority so clearly to remain with Hogarth, shall the mere contemptible difference of the scene of it being laid, in the one case, in our Fleet or King's Bench Prison, and, in the other, in the State Prison of Pisa, or the bedroom of a cardinal, —or that the subject of the one has never been authenticated, and the other is matter of history, —so weigh down the real points, of the comparison, as to induce us to rank the artist who has chosen the one scene or subject (though confessedly inferior in that which constitutes the soul of his art) in a class from which we exclude the better genius (who has happened to make choice of the other) with something like disgrace? [2]

[Footnote 1: The first perhaps in all Hogarth for serious expression. That which comes next to it, I think, is the jaded morning countenance of the debauchee in the second plate of the *Marriage Alamode*, which lectures on the vanity of pleasure as audibly as anything in Ecclesiastes. ]

[Footnote 2: Sir Joshua Reynolds, somewhere in his Lectures, speaks of the *presumption* of Hogarth in attempting the grand style in painting, by which he means his choice of certain Scripture subjects. Hogarth's excursions into Holy Land were not very numerous, but what he has left us in this kind have at least this merit, that they have expression of *some sort or other* in them, —the *Child Moses before Pharaoh's Daughter*, for instance: which is more than can be said of Sir Joshua Reynolds's *Repose in Egypt*, painted for Macklin's Bible, where for a Madonna he has substituted a sleepy, insensible, unmotherly girl, one so little worthy to have been selected as the Mother of the Saviour, that she seems to have neither heart nor feeling to entitle her to become a mother at all. But indeed the race of Virgin Mary painters seems to have been cut up, root and branch, at the Reformation. Our artists are too good Protestants to give life to that admirable commixture of maternal tenderness with reverential awe and wonder approaching to worship, with which the Virgin Mothers of L. da Vinci and Raphael (themselves by their divine countenances inviting men to worship) contemplate the union of the two natures in the person of their Heaven-born Infant. ]

*The Boys under Demoniacal Possession* of Raphael and Domenichino, by what law of classification are we bound to assign them to belong to the great style in painting, and to degrade into an inferior class the Rake of Hogarth when he is the Madman in the Bedlam scene? I am sure he is far more impressive than either. It is a face which no one that has seen can easily forget. There is the stretch of human suffering to the utmost endurance, severe bodily pain brought on by strong mental agony, the frightful, obstinate laugh of madness, —yet all so unforced and natural, that those who never were witness to madness in real life, think they see nothing but what is familiar to them in this face. Here are no tricks of distortion, nothing but the natural face of agony. This is high tragic painting, and we might as well deny to Shakspeare the honors of a great tragedian, because he has interwoven scenes of mirth with the serious business of his plays, as refuse to Hogarth the same praise for the two concluding scenes of the *Rake's Progress*, because of the Comic Lunatics[1] which he has thrown into the one, or the Alchymist that he has introduced in the other, who is paddling in the coals of his furnace, keeping alive the flames of vain hope within the very walls of the prison to which the vanity has conducted him, which have taught the darker lesson of extinguished hope to the desponding figure who is the principal person of the scene.

[Footnote 1:

"There are of madmen, as there are of tame,
All humor'd not alike. We have here some
So apish and fantastic, play with a feather;
And though 'twould grieve a soul to see God's image
So blemish'd and defac'd, yet do they act
Such antick and such pretty lunacies,
That, spite of sorrow, they will make you smile.
Others again we have, like angry lions,
Fierce as wild bulls, untameable as flies."
*Honest Whore*.]

It is the force of these kindly admixtures which assimilates the scenes of Hogarth and of Shakspeare to the drama of real life, where no such thing as pure tragedy is to be found; but merriment and infelicity, ponderous crime and feather-light vanity, like twiformed births, disagreeing complexions of one intertexture, perpetually unite to show forth motley spectacles to the world. Then it is that the poet or painter shows his art, when in the selection of these comic adjuncts he chooses such circumstances as shall relieve, contrast with, or fall into, without forming a violent opposition to his principal object. Who sees not that the Grave-digger in *Hamlet*, the Fool in *Lear*, have a kind of correspondency to, and fall in with, the subjects which they seem to interrupt: while the comic stuff in *Venice Preserved*, and the doggerel nonsense of the Cook and his poisoning associates in the *Rollo* of Beaumont and Fletcher, are pure, irrelevant, impertinent discords, —as bad as the quarrelling dog and cat under the table of the *Lord and the Disciples at Emmaus* of Titian?

Not to tire the reader with perpetual reference to prints which he may not be fortunate enough to possess, it may be sufficient to remark, that the same tragic cast of expression and incident, blended in some instances with a greater alloy of comedy, characterizes his other great work, the *Marriage Alamode*, as well as those less elaborate exertions of his genius, the prints called *Industry* and *Idleness, the Distrest Poet*, &c., forming, with the *Harlot's* and *Rake's Progresses*, the most considerable, if not the largest class of his productions, —enough surely to rescue Hogarth from the imputation of being a mere buffoon, or one whose general aim was only to *shake the sides*.

There remains a very numerous class of his performances, the object of which must be confessed to be principally comic. But in all of them will be found something to distinguish them from the droll productions of Bunbury and others. They have this difference, that we do not merely laugh at, we are led into long trains of reflection by them. In this respect they resemble the characters of Chaucer's *Pilgrims*, which have strokes of humor in them enough to designate them for the most part as comic, but our strongest feeling still is wonder at the comprehensiveness of genius which could crowd, as poet and painter have done, into one small canvas so many diverse yet cooperating materials.

The faces of Hogarth have not a mere momentary interest, as in caricatures, or those grotesque physiognomies which we sometimes catch a glance of in the street, and, struck with their whimsicality, wish for a pencil and the power to sketch them down; and forget them again as rapidly, —but they are permanent abiding ideas. Not the sports of nature, but her necessary eternal classes. We feel that we cannot part with any of them, lest a link should be broken.

It is worthy of observation, that he has seldom drawn a mean or insignificant countenance. [1] Hogarth's mind was eminently reflective; and, as it has been well observed of Shakspeare, that he has transfused his own poetical character into the persons of his drama (they are all more or less *poets*) Hogarth has impressed a *thinking character* upon the persons of his canvas. This remark must not be taken universally. The exquisite idiotism of the little gentleman in the bag and sword beating his drum in the print of the *Enraged Musician*, would of itself rise up against so sweeping an assertion. But I think it will be found to be true of the generality of his countenances. The knife-grinder and Jew flute-player in the plate just mentioned, may serve as instances instead of a thousand. They have intense thinking faces, though the purpose to which they are subservient by no means required it; but indeed it seems as if it was painful to Hogarth to contemplate mere vacancy or insignificance.

[Footnote 1: If there are any of that description, they are in his *Strolling Players*, a print which has been cried up by Lord Orford as the richest of his productions, and it may be, for what I know, in the mere lumber, the properties, and dead furniture of the scene, but in living character and expression it is (for Hogarth) lamentably poor and wanting; it is perhaps the only one of his performances at which we have a right to feel disgusted. ]

This reflection of the artist's own intellect from the faces of his characters, is one reason why the works of Hogarth, so much more than those of any other artist, are objects of meditation. Our intellectual natures love the mirror which gives them back their own likenesses. The mental eye will not bend long with delight upon vacancy.

Another line of eternal separation between Hogarth and the common painters of droll or burlesque subjects, with whom he is often confounded, is the sense of beauty, which in the most unpromising subjects seems never wholly to have deserted him. "Hogarth himself, " says Mr. Coleridge, [1] from whom I have borrowed this observation, speaking of a scene which took place at Ratzeburg, "never drew a more ludicrous distortion, both of attitude and physiognomy, than this effect occasioned: nor was there wanting beside it one of those beautiful female faces which the same Hogarth, *in whom the satirist never extinguished that love of beauty which belonged to him as a poet*, so often and so gladly introduces as the central figure in a crowd of humorous deformities, which figure (such is the power of true genius) neither acts nor is meant to act as a contrast; but diffuses through all and over each of the group a spirit of reconciliation and human kindness; and even when the attention is no longer consciously directed to the cause of this feeling, still blends its tenderness with our laughter: and *thus prevents the instructive* merriment at the whims of nature, or the foibles or humors of our fellow-men, from degenerating into the heart-poison of contempt or hatred. " To the beautiful females in Hogarth, which Mr. C. has pointed out, might be added, the frequent introduction of children (which Hogarth seems to have taken a particular delight in) into his pieces. They have a singular effect in giving tranquillity and a portion of their own innocence to the subject. The baby riding in its mother's lap in the *March to Finchley*, (its careless innocent face placed directly behind the intriguing time-furrowed countenance of the treason-plotting French priest, ) perfectly sobers the whole of that tumultuous scene. The boy mourner winding up his top with so much unpretending insensibility in the plate of the *Harlot's Funeral*, (the only thing in that assembly that is not a hypocrite, ) quiets and soothes the mind that has been disturbed at the sight of so much depraved man and woman kind.

[Footnote 1: *The Friend*, No. XVI. ]

I had written thus far, when I met with a passage in the writings of the late Mr. Barry, which, as it falls in with the *vulgar notion* respecting Hogarth, which this Essay has been employed in combating, I shall take the liberty to transcribe, with such remarks as may suggest themselves to me in the transcription; referring the reader for a full answer to that which has gone before.

> "Notwithstanding Hogarth's merit does undoubtedly entitle him to an honorable place among the artists, and that his little compositions, considered as so many dramatic representations, abounding with humor, character, and extensive observations on the various incidents of low, faulty, and vicious life, are very ingeniously brought together, and frequently tell their own story with more facility than is often found in many of the elevated and more noble inventions of Raphael and other great men; yet it must be honestly confessed, that in what is called knowledge of the figure, foreigners have justly observed, that Hogarth is often so raw and unformed, as hardly to deserve the name of an artist. But this capital defect is not often perceivable, as examples of the naked and of elevated nature but rarely occur in his subjects, which are for the most part filled with characters that in their nature tend to deformity; besides his figures are small, and the jonctures, and other difficulties of drawing that might occur in their limbs, are artfully

concealed with their clothes, rags, &c. But what would atone for all his defects, even if they were twice told, is his admirable fund of invention, ever inexhaustible in its resources; and his satire, which is always sharp and pertinent, and often highly moral, was (except in a few instances, where he weakly and meanly suffered his integrity to give way to his envy) seldom or never employed in a dishonest or unmanly way. Hogarth has been often imitated in his satirical vein, sometimes in his humorous: but very few have attempted to rival him in his moral walk. The line of art pursued by my very ingenious predecessor and brother Academician, Mr. Penny, is quite distinct from that of Hogarth, and is of a much more delicate and superior relish; he attempts the heart, and reaches it, whilst Hogarth's general aim is only to shake the sides; in other respects no comparison can be thought of, as Mr. Penny has all that knowledge of the figure and academical skill which the other wanted. As to Mr. Bunbury, who had so happily succeeded in the vein of humor and caricatura, he has for some time past altogether relinquished it, for the more amiable pursuit of beautiful nature: this, indeed, is not to be wondered at, when we recollect that he has, in Mrs. Bunbury, so admirable an exemplar of the most finished grace and beauty continually at his elbow. But (to say all that occurs to me on this subject) perhaps it may be reasonably doubted, whether the being much conversant with Hogarth's method of exposing meanness, deformity, and vice, in many of his works, is not rather a dangerous, or, at least, a worthless pursuit; which, if it does not find a false relish and a love of and search after satire and buffoonery in the spectator, is at least not unlikely to give him one. Life is short; and the little leisure of it is much better laid out upon that species of art which is employed about the amiable and the admirable, as it is more likely to be attended with better and nobler consequences to ourselves. These two pursuits in art may be compared with two sets of people with whom we might associate; if we give ourselves up to the Footes, the Kenricks, &c. we shall be continually busied and paddling in whatever is ridiculous, faulty, and vicious in life; whereas there are those to be found with whom we should be in the constant pursuit and study of all that gives a value and a dignity to human nature. " [Account of a Series of Pictures in the Great Boom of the Society of Arts, Manufactures, and

Commerce, at the Adelphi, by James Barry, R.A., Professor of Painting to the Royal Academy, reprinted in the last quarto edition of his works. ]

"— —It must be honestly confessed, that in what is called knowledge of the figure, foreigners have justly observed, " &c.

It is a secret well known to the professors of the art and mystery of criticism, to insist upon what they do not find in a man's works, and to pass over in silence what they do. That Hogarth did not draw the naked figure so well as Michael Angelo might be allowed, especially as "examples of the naked, " as Mr. Barry acknowledges, "rarely (he might almost have said never) occur in his subjects; " and that his figures under their draperies do not discover all the fine graces of an Antinoüs or an Apollo, may be conceded likewise; perhaps it was more suitable to his purpose to represent the average forms of mankind in the mediocrity (as Mr. Burke expresses it) of the age in which he lived: but that his figures in general, and in his best subjects, are so glaringly incorrect as is here insinuated, I dare trust my own eye so far as positively to deny the fact. And there is one part of the figure in which Hogarth is allowed to have excelled, which these foreigners seem to have overlooked, or perhaps calculating from its proportion to the whole (a seventh or an eighth, I forget which, ) deemed it of trifling importance; I mean the human face; a small part, reckoning by geographical inches, in the map of man's body, but here it is that the painter of expression must condense the wonders of his skill, even at the expense of neglecting the "jonctures and other difficulties of drawing in the limbs, " which it must be a cold eye that, in the interest so strongly demanded by Hogarth's countenances, has leisure to survey and censure.

"The line of art pursued by my very ingenious predecessor and brother Academician, Mr. Penny. "

The first impression caused in me by reading this passage was an eager desire to know who this Mr. Penny was. This great surpasser of Hogarth in the "delicacy of his relish, " and the "line which he pursued, " where is he, what are his works, what has he to show? In vain I tried to recollect, till by happily putting the question to a friend who is more conversant in the works of the illustrious obscure than myself, I learnt that he was the painter of a *Death of Wolfe* which missed the prize the year that the celebrated picture of West on the same subject obtained it; that he also made a picture of the *Marquis of Granby relieving a Sick Soldier*; moreover, that he was the inventor of two pictures of *Suspended and Restored Animation*, which I now remember to have seen in the Exhibition some years since, and the prints from which are still extant in good men's houses. This, then, I suppose, is the line of subjects in which Mr. Penny was so much superior to Hogarth. I confess I am not of that opinion. The relieving of poverty by the purse, and the restoring a young man to his parents by using the methods prescribed by the Humane Society, are doubtless very amiable subjects, pretty things to teach the first rudiments of humanity; they amount to about as much instruction as the stories of good boys that give away their custards to poor beggar-boys in children's books. But, good God! is this *milk for babes* to be set up in opposition to Hogarth's moral scenes, his *strong meat for men*? As well might we prefer the fulsome verses upon their own goodness to which the gentlemen of the Literary Fund annually sit still with such shameless patience to listen, to the satires of Juvenal and Persius; because the former are full of tender images of Worth relieved by Charity, and Charity stretching out her hand to rescue sinking Genius, and the theme of the latter is men's crimes and follies with their black consequences—forgetful meanwhile of those strains of moral pathos, those sublime heart-touches, which these poets (in *them* chiefly showing themselves poets) are perpetually darting across the otherwise appalling gloom of their subject—consolatory remembrancers, when their pictures of guilty mankind have made us even to despair for our species, that there is such a thing as virtue and moral dignity in the world, that her unquenchable spark is not utterly out—refreshing admonitions, to which we turn for shelter from the too great heat and asperity of the general satire.

And is there nothing analogous to this in Hogarth? nothing which "attempts and reaches the heart?"—no aim beyond that of "shaking the sides?"—If the kneeling ministering female in the last scene of the *Rake's Progress*, the Bedlam scene, of which I have spoken before, and have dared almost to parallel it with the most absolute idea of Virtue which Shakspeare has left us, be not enough to disprove the assertion; if the sad endings of the Harlot and the Rake, the passionate heart-bleeding entreaties for forgiveness which the adulterous wife is pouring forth to her assassinated and dying lord in the last scene but one of the *Marriage Alamode*, —if these be not things to touch the heart, and dispose the mind to a meditative tenderness: is there nothing sweetly conciliatory in the mild patient face and gesture with which the wife seems to allay and ventilate the feverish irritated feelings of her poor poverty-distracted mate (the true copy of the *genus irritabile*), in the print of the *Distrest Poet*? or if an image of maternal love be required, where shall we find a sublimer view of it than in that aged woman in *Industry and Idleness* (plate V. ) who is clinging with the fondness of hope not quite extinguished to her brutal vice-hardened child, whom she is accompanying to the ship which is to bear him away from his native soil, of which he has been adjudged unworthy: in whose shocking face every trace of the human countenance seems obliterated, and a brute beast's to be left instead, shocking and repulsive to all but her who watched over it in its cradle before it was so sadly altered, and feels it must belong to her while a pulse by the vindictive laws of his country shall be suffered to continue to beat in it. Compared with such things, what is Mr. Penny's "knowledge of the figure and academical skill which Hogarth wanted? "

With respect to what follows concerning another gentleman, with the congratulations to him on his escape out of the regions of "humor and caricatura, " in which it appears he was in danger of travelling side by side with Hogarth, I can only congratulate my country, that Mrs. Hogarth knew *her* province better than, by disturbing her husband at his palette, to divert him from that universality of subject, which has stamped him perhaps, next to Shakspeare, the most inventive genius which this island has produced, into the "amiable pursuit of beautiful nature, " *i. e.*, copying ad infinitum the individual charms and graces of Mrs. H. "Hogarth's method of exposing meanness, deformity, and vice, paddling in whatever is ridiculous, faulty, and vicious. "

A person unacquainted with the works thus stigmatized would be apt to imagine that in Hogarth there was nothing else to be found but subjects of the coarsest and most repulsive nature. That his imagination was naturally unsweet, and that he delighted in raking into every species of moral filth. That he preyed upon sore places only, and took a pleasure in exposing the unsound and rotten parts of human nature: —whereas, with the exception of some of the plates of the *Harlot's Progress*, which are harder in their character than any of the rest of his productions (the *Stages of Cruelty* I omit as mere worthless caricatures, foreign to his general habits, the offspring of his fancy in some wayward humor), there is scarce one of his pieces where vice is most strongly satirized, in which some figure is not introduced upon which the moral eye may rest satisfied;

a face that indicates goodness, or perhaps mere good-humoredness and carelessness of mind (negation of evil) only, yet enough to give a relaxation to the frowning brow of satire, and keep the general air from tainting. Take the mild, supplicating posture of patient Poverty in the poor woman that is persuading the pawnbroker to accept her clothes in pledge, in the plate of *Gin Lane*, for an instance. A little does it, a little of the *good* nature overpowers a world of *bad*. One cordial honest laugh of a Tom Jones absolutely clears the atmosphere that was reeking with the black putrefying breathings of a hypocrite Blifil. One homely expostulating shrug from Strap warms the whole air which the suggestions of a gentlemanly ingratitude from his friend Random had begun to freeze. One "Lord bless us! " of Parson Adams upon the wickedness of the times, exorcises and purges off the mass of iniquity which the world-knowledge of even a Fielding could cull out and rake together. But of the severer class of Hogarth's performances, enough, I trust, has been said to show that they do not merely shock and repulse; that there is in them the "scorn of vice" and the "pity" too; something to touch the heart, and keep alive the sense of moral beauty; the "lacrymæ rerum, " and the sorrowing by which the heart is made better. If they be bad things, then is satire and tragedy a bad thing; let us proclaim at once an age of gold, and sink the existence of vice and misery in our speculations: let us

"— —wink, and shut our apprehensions up
From common sense of what men were and are:"

let us *make believe* with the children, that everybody is good and happy; and, with Dr. Swift, write panegyrics upon the world.

But that larger half of Hogarth's works, which were painted more for entertainment than instruction (though such was the suggestiveness of his mind that there is always something to be learnt from them), his humorous scenes, —are they such as merely to disgust and set us against our species?

The confident assertions of such a man as I consider the late Mr. Barry to have been, have that weight of authority in them which staggers at first hearing, even a long preconceived opinion. When I read his pathetic admonition concerning the shortness of life, and how much better the little leisure of it were laid out upon "that species of art which is employed about the amiable and the admirable; " and Hogarth's "method, " proscribed as a "dangerous or worthless pursuit, " I began to think there was something in it;

that I might have been indulging all my life a passion for the works of this artist, to the utter prejudice of my taste and moral sense; but my first convictions gradually returned, a world of good-natured English faces came up one by one to my recollection, and a glance at the matchless *Election Entertainment*, which I have the happiness to have hanging up in my parlor, subverted Mr. Barry's whole theory in an instant.

In that inimitable print (which in my judgment as far exceeds the more known and celebrated *March to Finchley*, as the best comedy exceeds the best farce that ever was written), let a person look till he be saturated, and when he has done wondering at the inventiveness of genius which could bring so many characters (more than thirty distinct classes of face) into a room and set them down at table together, or otherwise dispose them about, in so natural a manner, engage them in so many easy sets and occupations, yet all partaking of the spirit of the occasion which brought them together, so that we feel that nothing but an election time could have assembled them; having no central figure or principal group, (for the hero of the piece, the Candidate, is properly set aside in the levelling indistinction of the day, one must look for him to find him, ) nothing to detain the eye from passing from part to part, where every part is alike instinct with life, —for here are no furniture-faces, no figures brought in to fill up the scene like stage choruses, but all dramatis personæ; when he shall have done wondering at all these faces so strongly charactered, yet finished with the accuracy of the finest miniature; when he shall have done admiring the numberless appendages of the scene, those gratuitous doles which rich genius flings into the heap when it has already done enough, the over-measure which it delights in giving, as if it felt its stores were exhaustless; the dumb rhetoric of the scenery, —for tables, and chairs, and joint-stools in Hogarth are living and significant things; the witticisms that are expressed by words (all artists but Hogarth have failed when they have endeavored to combine two mediums of expression, and have introduced words into their pictures), and the unwritten numberless little allusive pleasantries that are scattered about; the work that is going on in the scene, and beyond it, as is made visible to the "eye of mind, " by the mob which chokes up the doorway, and the sword that has forced an entrance before its master; when he shall have sufficiently admired this wealth of genius, let him fairly say what is the *result* left on his mind. Is it an impression of the vileness and worthlessness of his species? or is it not the general feeling which remains, after the individual faces have ceased to act sensibly on his mind, a *kindly one in favor of his species?* was not the general air of the scene wholesome? did it do the heart hurt to be among it? Something of a riotous spirit to be sure is there, some worldly-mindedness in some of the faces, a Doddingtonian smoothness which does not promise any superfluous degree of sincerity in the fine gentleman who has been the occasion of calling so much good company together; but is not the general cast of expression in the faces of the good sort? do they not seem cut out of the *good old rock*, substantial English honesty? would one fear treachery among characters of their expression? or shall we call their honest mirth and seldom-returning relaxation by the hard names of vice and profligacy? That poor country fellow, that is grasping his staff (which, from that difficulty of feeling themselves at home which poor men experience at a feast, he has never parted with since he came into the room), and is enjoying with a relish that seems to fit all the capacities of his soul the slender joke, which that facetious wag his neighbor is practising upon the gouty gentleman, whose eyes the effort to suppress pain has made as round as rings—does it shock the "dignity of human nature" to look at that man, and to sympathize with him in the seldom-heard joke which has unbent his careworn, hard-working visage, and drawn iron smiles from it? or with that full-hearted cobbler, who is honoring with the grasp of an honest fist the unused palm of that annoyed patrician, whom the license of the time has seated next him?

I can see nothing "dangerous" in the contemplation of such scenes as this, or the *Enraged Musician*, or the *Southwark Fair*, or twenty other pleasant prints which come crowding in upon my recollection, in which the restless activities, the diversified bents and humors, the blameless peculiarities of men, as they deserve to be called, rather than their "vices and follies, " are held up in a laughable point of view. All laughter is not of a dangerous or soul-hardening tendency. There is the petrifying sneer of a demon which excludes and kills Love, and there is the cordial laughter of a man which implies and cherishes it. What heart was ever made the worse by joining in a hearty laugh at the simplicities of Sir Hugh Evans or Parson Adams, where a sense of the ridiculous mutually kindles and is kindled by a perception of the amiable? That tumultuous harmony of singers that are roaring out the words, "The world shall bow to the Assyrian throne, " from the opera of *Judith*, in the third plate of the series called the *Four Groups of Heads*; which the quick eye of Hogarth must have struck off in the very infancy of the rage for sacred oratorios in this country, while "Music yet was young; " when we have done smiling at the deafening distortions, which these tearers of devotion to rags and tatters, these takers of heaven by storm, in their boisterous mimicry of the occupation of angels, are making, —what unkindly impression is left behind, or what more of harsh or contemptuous feeling, than when we quietly leave Uncle Toby and Mr. Shandy riding their hobby-horses about the room? The conceited, long-backed Sign-painter, that with all the self-applause of a Raphael or Correggio, (the twist of body which his conceit has thrown him into has something of the Correggiesque in it, ) is contemplating the picture of a bottle, which he is drawing from an actual bottle that hangs beside him, in the print of *Beer Street*, — while we smile at the enormity of the self-delusion, can we help loving the good-humor and self-complacency of the fellow? would we willingly wake him from his dream?

I say not that all the ridiculous subjects of Hogarth have, necessarily, something in them to make us like them; some are indifferent to us, some in their natures repulsive, and only made interesting by the wonderful skill and truth to nature in the painter; but I contend that there is in most of them that sprinkling of the better nature, which, like holy water, chases away and disperses the contagion of the bad. They have this in them, besides, that they bring us acquainted with the every-day human face, —they give us skill to detect those gradations of sense and virtue (which escape the careless or fastidious observer) in the countenances of the world about us; and prevent that disgust at common life, that *tædium quotidianarum formarum*, which an unrestricted passion for ideal forms and beauties is in danger of producing. In this, as in many other things, they are analogous to the best novels of Smollett or Fielding.

\* \* \* \* \*

# Essays

## ON THE POETICAL WORKS OF GEORGE WITHER

The poems of G. Wither are distinguished by a hearty homeliness of manner, and a plain moral speaking. He seems to have passed his life in one continued act of an innocent self-pleasing. That which he calls his *Motto* is a continued self-eulogy of two thousand lines, yet we read it to the end without any feeling of distaste, almost without a consciousness that we have been listening all the while to a man praising himself. There are none of the cold particles in it, the hardness and self-ends, which render vanity and egotism hateful. He seems to be praising another person, under the mask of self: or rather, we feel that it was indifferent to him where he found the virtue which he celebrates; whether another's bosom or his own were its chosen receptacle. His poems are full, and this in particular is one downright confession, of a generous self-seeking. But by self he sometimes means a great deal, —his friends, his principles, his country, the human race.

Whoever expects to find in the satirical pieces of this writer any of those peculiarities which pleased him in the satires of Dryden or Pope, will be grievously disappointed. Here are no high-finished characters, no nice traits of individual nature, few or no personalities. The game run down is coarse general vice, or folly as it appears in classes. A liar, a drunkard, a coxcomb, is *stript and whipt;* no Shaftesbury, no Villiers, or Wharton, is curiously anatomized, and read upon. But to a well-natured mind there is a charm of moral sensibility running through them, which amply compensates the want of those luxuries. Wither seems everywhere bursting with a love of goodness, and a hatred of all low and base actions. At this day it is hard to discover what parts of the poem here particularly alluded to, *Abuses Stript and Whipt*, could have occasioned the imprisonment of the author. Was Vice in High Places more suspicious than now? had she more power; or more leisure to listen after ill reports? That a man should be convicted of a libel when he named no names but Hate, and Envy, and Lust, and Avarice, is like one of the indictments in the Pilgrim's Progress, where Faithful is arraigned for having "railed on our noble Prince Beelzebub, and spoken contemptibly of his honorable friends, the Lord Old Man, the Lord Carnal Delight, and the Lord Luxurious. " What unlucky jealousy could have tempted the great men of those days to appropriate such innocent abstractions to themselves?

Wither seems to have contemplated to a degree of idolatry his own possible virtue. He is forever anticipating persecution and martyrdom; fingering, as it were, the flames, to try how he can bear them. Perhaps his premature defiance sometimes made him obnoxious to censures which he would otherwise have slipped by.

The homely versification of these Satires is not likely to attract in the present day. It is certainly not such as we should expect from a poet "soaring in the high region of his fancies, with his garland and his singing robes about him; "[1] nor is it such as he has shown in his *Philarete*, and in some parts of his *Shepherds Hunting*. He seems to have adopted this dress with voluntary humility, as fittest for a moral teacher, as our divines choose sober gray or black; but in their humility consists their sweetness. The deepest tone of moral feeling in them (though all throughout is weighty, earnest, and passionate) is in those pathetic injunctions against shedding of blood in quarrels, in the chapter entitled *Revenge*. The story of his own forbearance, which follows, is highly interesting. While the Christian sings his own victory over Anger, the Man of Courage cannot help peeping out to let you know, that it was some higher principle than *fear* which counselled this forbearance.

[Footnote 1: Milton. ]

Whether encaged, or roaming at liberty, Wither never seems to have abated a jot of that free spirit which sets its mark upon his writings, as much as a predominant feature of independence impresses every page of our late glorious Burns; but the elder poet wraps his proof-armor closer about him, the other wears his too much outwards; he is thinking too much of annoying the foe to be quite easy within; the spiritual defences of Wither are a perpetual source of inward sunshine, the magnanimity of the modern is not without its alloy of soreness, and a sense of injustice, which seems perpetually to gall and irritate. Wither was better skilled in the "sweet uses of adversity; " he knew how to extract the "precious jewel" from the head of the "toad, " without drawing any of the "ugly venom" along with it. The prison-notes of Wither are finer than the wood-notes of most of his poetical brethren. The description in the Fourth Eclogue of his *Shepherds Hunting* (which was composed during his imprisonment in the Marshalsea) of the power of the Muse to extract pleasure from common objects, has been oftener quoted, and is more known, than any part of his writings. Indeed, the whole Eclogue is in a strain so much above not only what himself, but almost what any other poet has written, that he himself could not help noticing it; he remarks that his spirits had been raised higher than they were wont, "through the love of poesy. " The praises of Poetry have been often sung in ancient and in modern times; strange powers have been ascribed to it of influence over animate and inanimate auditors; its force over fascinated crowds has been acknowledged; but, before Wither, no one ever celebrated its power *at home*, the wealth and the strength which this divine gift confers upon its possessor. Fame, and that too after death, was all which hitherto the poets had promised themselves from their art. It seems to have been left to Wither to discover that poetry was a present possession, as well as a rich reversion, and that the Muse had promise of both lives, —of this, and of that which was to come.

The *Mistress of Philarete* is in substance a panegyric protracted through several thousand lines in the mouth of a single speaker, but diversified, so as to produce an almost dramatic effect, by the artful introduction of some ladies, who are rather auditors than interlocutors in the scene; and of a boy, whose singing furnishes pretence for an occasional change of metre: though the seven-syllable line, in which the main part of it is written, is that in which Wither has shown himself so great a master, that I do not know that I am always thankful to him for the exchange.

Wither has chosen to bestow upon the lady whom he commends the name of Arete, or Virtue; and, assuming to himself the character of Philarete, or Lover of Virtue, there is a sort of propriety in that heaped measure of perfections which he attributes to this partly real, partly allegorical personage. Drayton before him had shadowed his mistress under the name of Idea, or Perfect Pattern, and some of the old Italian love-strains are couched in such religious terms as to make it doubtful whether it be a mistress, or Divine Grace, which the poet is addressing.

In this poem (full of beauties) there are two passages of preeminent merit. The first is where the lover, after a flight of rapturous commendation, expresses his wonder why all men that are about his mistress, even to her very servants, do not view her with the same eyes that he does.

"Sometime I do admire
All men burn not with desire:
Nay, I muse her servants are not

Pleading love; but 0! they dare not.
And I therefore wonder, why
They do not grow sick and die.
Sure they would do so, but that,
By the ordinance of fate,
There is some concealed thing,
So each gazer limiting,
He can see no more of merit,
Than beseems his worth and spirit.
For in her a grace there shines,
That o'er-daring thoughts confines,
Making worthless men despair
To be loved of one so fair.
Yea, the destinies agree,
Some *good judgments* blind should be,
And not gain the power of knowing
Those rare beauties in her growing.
Reason doth as much imply:
For, if every judging eye,
Which beholdeth her, should there
Find what excellences are,
All, o'ercome by those perfections,
Would be captive to affections.
So, in happiness unblest,
She for lovers should not rest."

The other is, where he has been comparing her beauties to gold, and stars, and the most excellent things in nature; and, fearing to be accused of hyperbole, the common charge against poets, vindicates himself by boldly taking upon him, that these comparisons are no hyperboles; but that the best things in nature do, in a lover's eye, fall short of those excellences which he adores in her.

"What pearls, what rubies can
Seem so lovely fair to man,
As her lips whom he doth love,
When in sweet discourse they move,
Or her lovelier teeth, the while
She doth bless him with a smile?
Stars indeed fair creatures be;
Yet amongst us where is he
Joys not more the whilst he lies
Sunning in his mistress' eyes,

Than in all the glimmering light
Of a starry winter's night?
Note the beauty of an eye—
And if aught you praise it by
Leave such passion in your mind,
Let my reason's eye be blind.
Mark if ever red or white
Any where gave such delight,
As when they have taken place
In a worthy woman's face.

\* \* \* \* \*

"I must praise her as I may,
Which I do mine own rude way,
Sometimes setting forth her glories
By unheard of allegories "—&c.

To the measure in which these lines are written the wits of Queen Anne's days contemptuously gave the name of Namby-Pamby, in ridicule of Ambrose Philips, who has used it in some instances, as in the lines on Cuzzoni, to my feeling at least, very deliciously; but Wither, whose darling measure it seems to have been, may show, that in skilful hands it is capable of expressing the subtilest movements of passion. So true it is, which Drayton seems to have felt, that it is the poet who modifies the metre, not the metre the poet; in his own words, that

  "It's possible to climb;
To kindle, or to stake;
  Altho' in Skelton's rhime."[1]

[Footnote 1: A long line is a line we are long repeating. In the *Shepherds Hunting* take the following—

"If thy verse doth bravely tower,
*As she makes wing, she gets power;*
Yet the higher she doth soar,
She's affronted still the more,
'Till she to the high'st hath past,
Then she rests with fame at last."

Essays

What longer measure can go beyond the majesty of this! what Alexandrine is half so long in pronouncing or expresses *labor slowly but strongly surmounting difficulty* with the life with which it is done in the second of these lines? or what metre could go beyond these from *Philarete*—

"Her true beauty leaves behind
Apprehensions in my mind
Of more sweetness, than all art
Or inventions can impart.
*Thoughts too deep to be expressed,*
*And too strong to be suppressed."*]

CPSIA information can be obtained
at www.ICGtesting.com
Printed in the USA
LVHW102202090522
718369LV00005B/199

9 781406 549096